CW00766979

asian greens

ANITA LOH-YIEN LAU

asian greens

A COOK'S GUIDE

APPLE

DEDICATION
This book is dedicated with all my love to my mother, Barbara who has inspired
and encouraged me to become who I am today.

A QUINTET BOOK

Published by
Apple Press
Sheridan House
112-116A Western Road
Hove
East Sussex BN3 1DD

ISBN 1-84092-345-8

This book was designed and produced by
Quintet Publishing Limited
6 Blundell Street
London N7 9BH

EDITORIAL DIRECTOR: Jeremy Harwood

MANAGING EDITOR: Toria Leitch

EDITOR: Debbie Foy

CREATIVE DIRECTOR: Richard Dewing

ART DIRECTOR: Sharanjit Dhol

PHOTOGRAPHY: Ian Garlick, Paola Zucchi,
Salima Hirani

FOOD STYLIST: Kathryn Hawkins

DESIGNER: Deep Creative

The Publisher would like to thank the following for help with photography in
Hong Kong's street markets:
The family at 16a Bowrington Road, Causeway Bay, Hong Kong; Annie Yuen; and Kan
Kwok Hung at Fu Tung Market, Tung Chung, Hong Kong.

Manufactured in Hong Kong / Printed in China

CONTENTS

INTRODUCTION

WHEN I SET OUT TO WRITE THIS BOOK, MY FIRST INSTINCT WAS THAT THERE WOULD NEVER BE ENOUGH GREEN ASIAN VEGETABLES TO WRITE ABOUT. AFTER ALL, HOW MANY VARIETIES OF GREEN LEAFY VEGETABLES ARE THERE WHICH ARE EXCLUSIVELY ASIAN? GROWING UP IN HONG KONG AND MALAYSIA I WAS SURROUNDED BY AN ABUNDANCE OF ASIAN VEGETABLES, WHICH I ACCEPTED AS COMMONPLACE. THESE DAYS I REALIZE JUST HOW FEW PEOPLE IN THE WEST HAVE SEEN, LET ALONE SAMPLED, MANY OF THE VARIETIES OF VEGETABLE THAT ARE NOW, IN FACT, READILY AVAILABLE AROUND THE WORLD.

My intention in writing this book is to demystify the wealth of exotic vegetables so that you, the reader and cook, will feel confident to experiment with a leafy head of bok choy, a shiny bottle gourd or a spiky kohlrabi, to create authentic, flavoursome and nutritious dishes from anywhere across this fascinating continent. With that in mind, I decided to take some time to reflect upon my cultural and culinary experiences and produce a book with wide appeal, to capture the imagination of the seasoned Asian cook or the novice in Asian cuisine.

Traditional Asian families do not show affection as western families do, preferring to show love and care through food. Eating is therefore an integral part of the Asian family. The recipes I have included here are some of my family and friends' favourites. Many are my mother's recipes, some you might recognize as traditional Asian favourites and others are dishes I have tasted on my travels. Every recipe has been adapted at one time or another to suit my needs or simply because an ingredient was not available at the time.

Some of the condiments I have used in my recipes may not be staples in your larder but are usually readily available in your local Asian grocery store. For your convenience, I have also included authentic recipes for sambal oelek (chilli sauce) and kecap manis (sweet soy sauce) as they are simple to make and keep well. I am unable to provide names of my favourite brands here, but I suggest you shop around, try out several and find the one you like best. With use you will become familiar with the basic sauces and spices of Asian cooking and they will no longer be an exotic touch, but a welcome necessity.

FOOD IS WHAT HOLDS THE ASIAN FAMILY TOGETHER

As well as the green vegetables and herbs, I have also included some roots, fruits and other ingredients commonly used in Asian cuisine. The recipes are health-conscious, easy to follow, and not too time consuming. Some can also be adapted to suit the less adventurous palate. Cooking and eating Asian food is all about sharing and a sense of communality and togetherness. Asian food is most pleasurable when shared with family and friends and I recommend you prepare at least three to four dishes for four people to share.

The next time you visit your Asian grocery store take home a bunch of chrysanthemum leaves or water spinach and experiment with it. Or throw a couple of Asian herbs into a pot of soup to spice it up. You may be surprised by the subtle, fresh or unique flavours you will discover and you may find that your cooking is never the same again!

ESSENTIAL CONDIMENTS

IN MY RECIPES I USE A CORE OF ITEMS SUCH AS SOY SAUCE, FISH SAUCE AND COOKING WINE, WHICH I CONSIDER TO BE THE STAPLES OF THE ASIAN KITCHEN. A GOOD ASIAN GROCERY STORE OR SUPERMARKET WILL USUALLY STOCK A VAST RANGE OF BASIC INGREDIENTS BUT THE KEY TO FINDING THOSE THAT SUIT YOU BEST IS SIMPLY TO EXPERIMENT. ENJOY!

Traditional soy sauce from Japan is excellent for dipping and cooking, but I prefer Chinese soy sauces, which come in light and dark varieties, for marinating meats. Dark soy sauce has molasses added to give it a richer colour, making it perfect for barbecue marinades and glazes. Other indispensable condiments are Chinese oyster sauce, Japanese sweet rice wine, Japanese rice vinegar, Thai red or green curry paste, coconut milk, Chinese cooking wine and oyster sauce—a pricier one is worth the expense. As to fish sauce, I find the Thai varieties more flavoursome than those from the Philippines.

IN THE PAST PEOPLE WOULD PREPARE THEIR OWN SAUCE

Japanese sweet rice wine or *mirin* is a staple. The cheaper versions labelled 'sweet sauce for cooking' are best avoided as they have no alcohol in them but are instead laden with corn syrup or fructose. Rice vinegar is also a useful addition to your store cupboard but I find cider vinegar works just as well.

Dashi, a Japanese stock made with kelp and bonito flakes, is an essential ingredient in authentic Japanese cooking. You can make your own, however, if you do not have the time for this, use the stock granules (*dashi-no-moto*) sold in Asian grocery stores. I use a pre-prepared brand of *dashi-no-moto* when short of time, but the granules contain monosodium glutamate (MSG) and other additives such as lactose and sugar, so be aware if you are sensitive or allergic to food additives. If you buy instant dashi and the instructions turn out to be in Japanese use the following method: in a pan, stir 1 heaped teaspoon of granules into 20 fl oz/568 ml cold water and bring to the boil.

Prepared jars of Thai red and green curry pastes are an excellent basic to add to your store cupboard, as is high-quality tinned coconut milk. By substituting light coconut milk, you will substantially lower saturated fats in your cooking without reducing the flavours too much. I often use Shaoxing wine in my marinades, but I find dry sherry does just as well. Yellow bean, hoisin and black bean sauces are also good to have in stock. In the past people would prepare their own sauce but these days the available brand sauces are very authentic.

GREENS GUIDE

LEAFY AND FLOWERING GREENS

A-CHOY
Mak choy

Very popular in its native Taiwan, a-choy is now widely available in Asian grocery stores in the west. Resembling Romaine lettuce leaves, a-choy has long tapered yellowish-green leaves and is highly perishable so should be consumed as soon as it is purchased. Although it is often difficult to find a lively bunch of a-choy as the leaves wilt very quickly, choose the firmest bunch available. Perfect for flash frying and stir fries, its texture is very delicate and crisp with a rather refreshing taste. In Taiwan it is generally flash fried with a bit of oil and garlic, but even if you stir fry it a little too long, its texture still remains crunchy and totally delectable.

SNOW PEA SHOOTS
Dau miu

There are two kinds of snow pea shoots, one with large leaves (dai dau miu) and one with small leaves (sai dau miu). The former are the leaves and tender tips of the vines on which snow peas grow. These are delicate and tasty and best used when freshly picked, otherwise they lose their sweetness. The smaller pea shoots, which look more like sprouts, have a different texture and taste. Most food critics will tell you that the smaller sprout-like shoots are inferior, but I think both have something to offer. Both types should be eaten right away, preferably on the day of purchase. Choose fresh-looking leaves which have not yet wilted.

MIZUNA
Kyona, King choy

A pot herb, mizuna is indigenous to Japan and is part of the mustard family. Generally used as a garnish in Japanese cuisine, its earthy, fresh taste is excellent raw in salads, steamed and served as a side dish with a splash of dressing or stir-fried with various meats. Its attractive leaf is similar in size to rocket with a feathery appearance and soft jagged edges. Traditionally used in Asian hotpots, mizuna has succulent white stalks and its leaves have a hint of mustard. Fresh mizuna can be stored in the refrigerator for up to two days in a plastic bag.

AMARANTH

Yeen choy, Hsien, Marsa, Tamri bhaji, Lol cholai, Jacob's coat

From the family of leaf amaranths, this vegetable grows on a slender stem with oval-shaped, slightly rough-textured leaves growing in clusters. It has light or dark green leaves or a green leaf with deep red veins sometimes known as Ganges amaranth, red amaranth, red saag or red spinach. The leaves are fragile and wilt easily so it should be cooked right away. Amaranth tastes like spinach, which makes an acceptable substitute, even though amaranth has more of an earthy flavour. When buying, choose sprightly looking leaves with roots intact. When using, discard the roots and tough lower stems and wash thoroughly as it has a lot of hidden dirt. In developing countries it is considered an important dietary aid as it is an extremely high source of protein, minerals and vitamin C.

BOK CHOY

Baby bok choy, Shanghai bok choy, Bok choy sum, Pak choi

This is the most widely known Asian vegetable in the west and also comes in different varieties. Bok choy comes in two sizes, both with dark green leaves on milky white stalks. The shorter version is known as baby bok choy. My favourite is Shanghai bok choy, the winter variety of bok choy, which is smaller in size with pale green spoon-shaped stalks. Bok choy sum is similar in flavour but has yellow flowers like the choy sum. Since there is only a slight difference in taste, they can all be interchanged when cooking. Choose unblemished leaves with firm stalks and no limpness. Very fresh bok choy will keep for three to four days in the refrigerator wrapped in kitchen paper.

BAMBOO MUSTARD GREENS

Bamboo mustard cabbage, Juk gai choy

Similar in appearance to other Asian mustard greens but looks very different from western cabbage or mustard greens. There are many varieties of Asian mustard greens, and this particular variety boasts thin, pale green stalks with sawtooth-edged leaves and takes longer to cook than other varieties. It is recommended that you boil this vegetable for a few minutes before using it in dishes. Its taste resembles western mustard greens and can be used as a substitute. It will keep in the refrigerator for four to five days in a plastic bag.

INDIAN LETTUCE
Tong sang choy

Despite its name, Indian lettuce is actually from China. Tong sang choy means Chinese lettuce and it is grown mainly for its leaves and used as a vegetable. Its leaves are in shape similar to Romaine lettuce but slightly wider with fuller, light green leaves. Although it tastes like a-choy, it is not as crisp in texture, and is not as bland as the crisphead lettuce. Choose and store as you would Romaine lettuce. Can be substituted with Romaine or iceberg lettuce.

KOMATSUNA
Mustard spinach

From the brassica family, komatsuna has smooth, light green leaves and looks a little like small choy sum without the yellow flowers. Although it is referred to as a spinach, it is more like a leafy turnip. Its flavour is crisp and refreshing, similar to choy sum but with a more subtle taste. It is known as purely a Japanese vegetable, and is now readily available in Japanese shops, sold in bunches. Rich in calcium, komatsuna does not keep well and should be consumed immediately, either raw or parboiled.

LETTUCE STEM
Celtuce, Asparagus lettuce, Wo sun

A close relative of wild lettuce, celtuce, or lettuce stem is cultivated for its tender stem rather than its leaves. Easily distinguishable by its long, light green stem marked with brown rings where the leaves have fallen off, its leaves are added to soups, while its stem is used in a variety of ways. It has a crunchy texture and a natural fresh flavour, reminiscent of mild celery and is used in salads or parboiled as a side dish. Store loosely wrapped in kitchen paper, in a plastic bag, for up to two weeks in the refrigerator.

FLAT CABBAGE
Rosette bok choy, Tatsoi, Tai koo choy

This variety of cabbage has thicker and darker leaves than the normal bok choy but displays the same white stem as the common bok choy. It often looks more like a floral bouquet than a vegetable. It tastes very like bok choy with a slightly stronger flavour and is great in salads. Rocket is a good substitute although tatsoi does not have the sweet hints of the salad leaf. Store and use as you would bok choy, but make sure you wash it thoroughly as it harbours a lot of dirt and grit.

CHRYSANTHEMUM LEAVES
Garland chrysanthemum, Tong ho, Shungiku

In Asia it is easy to tell when the weather turns cool as you will find chrysanthemum leaves abundant in the markets. A flowering vegetable with a subtle, musty floral aroma, chrysanthemum leaves are highly popular in Japan where they are used in soups or Chinese hotpots—a customary winter dining experience. Do not be alarmed if you can only find slightly wilted bunches, this is quite usual. It is a highly perishable vegetable so it is best to use it immediately. It is also one of the grittiest vegetables around so wash thoroughly and discard the buds before using. When cooked it changes from pale green to a deep dark green.

SWATOW MUSTARD GREENS
Chinese mustard greens, Wrapped heart mustard cabbage, Dai gai choy

From the brassica family, swatow mustard greens look like an elongated cabbage but with a slightly bulbous base and tightly packed jade green leaves at the top. Similar in taste to the bamboo mustard green, the swatow is much larger in size. It is most often used in pickling, in soups or in sharp, sour-tasting dishes.

DRUMSTICK LEAVES
Malongai, Kelor, Phak ma-rum, Sahjan, Saragova, Setka ni sing, Marungai

From a tree known as the horseradish tree, the leaves and pods are used in various Asian cuisines. The pods have a similar taste to horseradish while the leaves are generally used for their tangy flavour. In India the leaves are cooked with spices and shredded coconut while in Thailand they are blanched and dipped in nam prik (dipping sauce). Filipinos add drumstick leaves as a last-minute flavouring to sour soups. Choose fresh-looking leaves and green pods. They will keep a few days in the refrigerator, but are really best eaten right away. Rinse well under running water and shake off any excess water before using.

NAPA CABBAGE

Chinese cabbage, Celery cabbage, Tientsin cabbage, Michihili, Hakusai

These sweet creamy stalks with ruffled, pale green edges are now becoming more widely available everywhere. The large and slightly rounded variety is more common in the west, but the long thin variety can also be found in Asian grocery stores. These two types of firm, tightly packed heads are topped by crinkly edged leaves, and taste almost the same, so can be used interchangeably. Napa cabbage is more delicate in texture and taste than Savoy cabbage, and is preferred by those who find the common cabbage too strong. It also cooks in less time than the traditional cabbage and can be used raw or cooked. When selecting a napa cabbage avoid those whose leaves are already spotting. Napa cabbage should be stored as you would lettuce and generally keeps extremely well in the refrigerator, sometimes for up to three weeks.

OIL SEED RAPE

Choy sum, Yau choy, Flowering cabbage

In appearance, choy sum looks very much like bok choy sum except the stalks are slim, of a light green colour and the leaves often display pretty yellow edible flowers. The taste is milder than gai lan and the texture less crunchy when cooked for the same amount of time as gai lan. Use as you would broccoli raab (rapini). When buying choose firm, thin stalks with large, flourishing leaves with no brown spots. Droopy leaves suggest it has been sitting around for a while. Use as soon as possible since the longer you keep it, the less texture it will have after cooking. When using wash thoroughly and shake off any excess water. Oil seed rape will keep for two to three days in the refrigerator if very fresh.

MALABAR SPINACH

Indian spinach, Slippery vegetable, Vine spinach, Saan choy, Alogbati

An Indian spinach with dark green, round or oval leaves, this particular variety has a very strong, earthy spinach flavour and a slippery texture. Some people find its taste off-putting but it is rich in protein, vitamins and minerals. The best way to enjoy this vegetable is in a soup with pork. It will store for up to a week in the refrigerator.

CHINESE BROCCOLI
Gai lan, Gai lan fa, Chinese kale

An attractive dark, leafy green often with dark green buds and small, white edible flowers, gai lan looks and tastes very similar to broccoli raab (rapini), but without the bitterness. It has fuller leaves than broccoli raab and is relished for its firm emphatic flavour, and generally, only the leaves and tender portion of the stem are eaten. Chinese broccoli can sometimes taste spicy, often with a hint of mustard seed. When buying, look for dark green stalks with thick stems. Leaves should look young and tender, but most grown in the west are bound to have large, tough leaves. Discard the larger, tougher outer leaves leaving the medium to smaller leaves intact. Broccoli stems are acceptable substitutes but without the trademark mustard hints of gai lan. It will keep two to three days in the refrigerator when fresh. Cook as you would broccoli.

WATER SPINACH
Morning glory, Swamp cabbage, Ung choy, Tung choy, Pak boong, Rau muang

In Asia there are two types of water spinach, but in the west only one type is available. The water spinach sold in your Asian grocery store has long hollow stems and pointed arrowhead leaves. At a pinch, water spinach will keep for a day or two in the refrigerator, but really it does not keep well at all. Its leaves turn yellow and deteriorate very quickly. This versatile vegetable is used in almost every Asian cuisine I know, and the most common way to cook it is with garlic and a little shrimp paste, with or without chillies. If your local Asian store does not stock water spinach then silver beet and green chard make good substitutes.

TAIWAN BOK CHOY
Fengshan bok choy

The stems of this vegetable are reminiscent of bok choy, but its leaves are long and yellow-green resembling lettuce. It tastes like bok choy and you can cook it as you would any other bok choys. Choose firm, unblemished leaves and store in the refrigerator for three or four days wrapped in kitchen paper, if you are not using it right away.

HERBS

CELERY LEAF
Smallage, Chinese celery leaf, Heung kun, Tang o, Tong kun, Kinchay, Cutting celery

Chinese celery is often mistaken for Italian parsley at first glance. This is because this marsh plant has stalks about a third of the size of traditional celery. It is most often used in soups, stews or blanched and used in salads. Although it is technically an herb, the Chinese use it like a vegetable. Its flavour is far more intense than traditional celery and many cookbooks suggest western celery leaves as a suitable substitute, but I am dubious as there is just no comparison when it comes to flavour. It is sold in bunches and will keep a few days in the refrigerator wrapped in kitchen paper and stored in a plastic bag.

SHISO LEAF
Perilla, Japanese basil, Beefsteak plant

A Japanese herb used as a condiment or garnish as one would use basil. There are two types available: one green, the other reddish-purple in colour, although the latter is mostly used as a food colouring and for pickling. Found in Japanese grocery stores, shiso is sold in bunches of eight to ten leaves packed in a polystyrene tray and will keep for up to three days in the refrigerator when fresh. After that, it starts to wilt. Choose firm, bright green leaves with no brown spots.

CORIANDER
Chinese parsley, Cilantro, Heung choy, Yeen sai, Pak chee, Pak hom pom, Rau ngo

A sweet-flavoured herb with hints of caraway, lemon and sage that is used in almost all Asian cuisines, either raw or cooked. When buying cilantro, choose fresh, green, supple looking bouquets with as few brown leaves as possible. Lay the cilantro out on kitchen paper and allow it to air-dry for about 20 minutes. Then roll it in kitchen paper, seal in a plastic bag and it will keep for about four to five days in the refrigerator.

DILL
Pak si, Pak chi lao

Readily available, fresh dill has soft, delicate, fern-like leaves, long stems and umbrella-like flowers. Often confused with fennel tops, dill is delicious with fish and is sprinkled fresh in many western dishes. However, in Asian cooking dill is almost always cooked. It gives off a delightful aroma and adds flavour to sauces and seafood dishes. Dill is fragile and should be kept no more than two days in the refrigerator.

MITSUBA
Trefoil, Honewort

A relative of cilantro and parsley, mitsuba means 'three leaves' in Japanese and is generally added to soups and salads. It resembles Italian parsley and is sold in bunches of long, light green, trifoliate leaves. Generally, parsley is an acceptable substitute although its taste is more like a mild chervil. In texture, the two are very different. It is also a herb that can be added to soups or dishes at the last minute as it loses its flavour with prolonged cooking. When buying, choose a bunch with crisp leaves and stems. Found in Japanese stores, mitsuba will usually last for about four to five days in the refrigerator with its roots immersed in water and a plastic bag covering its leaves.

KAFFIR LIME
Bergamot, Makrut

This wild lime has green fruit and bumpy, green wrinkled skin. Its zest is used in curries, but the lime leaves are indispensable to Thai savoury cooking. Kaffir lime leaves are dark green and shiny, double lobed, and extremely aromatic with a perfume unlike any other citrus fruit. Fresh leaves freeze well, so try not to use dried leaves, if possible. I have found that the dried are inferior and can spoil your recipe rather than enhance it. When buying kaffir lime leaves, make sure they are completely green without any brown spots. Many cookbooks suggest substituting fresh lime zest for the kaffir lime, and citrus leaves for the kaffir lime leaves. Personally, I believe that there is no substitute when it comes to kaffir lime leaves.

RAU RAM
Vietnamese mint, Vietnamese cilantro, Cambodian mint, Hot mint, Laksa leaf, Daun laksa, Pak chi wietnam, Daun kesom

Although it is sometimes known as mint, this herb tastes more like cilantro than mint.
It has narrow, tapered green leaves, ribbed with a purple hue although not every leaf may have these distinguishing marks, even from the same stem. It has a strong, distinctive flavour, which is pungent with hints of pepper and mint. In Singapore and Malaysia rau ram is cooked in soups, while in Vietnam it is served with nearly every meal, eaten raw in salads or cooked in spring rolls. Its leaves are especially good in chicken and fish dishes. You can substitute rau ram with a combination of fresh cilantro and common mint or spearmint.

GALANGAL
Galingale, Kha, Rieng, Lengkuas, Laos

A close cousin of root ginger, galangal has a sharper, more citrus flavour, often with a hint of pine. It has less of a bite than ginger although its appearance is the same, with a pale, thin skin and darker circles. Most often, galangal is paler in colour than ginger and has pink shoots or tips.

WILD BETEL LEAF
La Lot

This herb is generally sold in a plastic bag in Asian grocery stores. It is a spicy and higly nutritious leaf of a vine related to the black pepper plant. Its large, round and crinkled leaf is used as a leafy green in soups or as a wrapping for spring rolls, and is a standard garnish in Vietnamese cuisine. Not every Asian store will stock it, but if you do chance upon it, give it a try. Choose supple, green leaves with no wilting or blemishing. Vine leaves are acceptable substitutes.

CURRY LEAF
Daun kari, Meetha neem

The curry leaf is to Asian cooking what the bay leaf is to western cooking. Its shiny, small pointed leaves are mostly used in southern Indian, Sri Lankan and Malaysian food. Indian shops sell fresh curry leaves in plastic bags. Take a whiff of the aroma that filters from the bag and, if you are a curry lover, your tastebuds will go into overdrive. Curry leaves are an added luxury to curries and although they keep well the fresher they are the better the flavours. If you do not use up all the leaves in one to two days, dry them out for future use. It is better than trying to store them fresh.

SHALLOTS

These are similar to onions but have a more intense flavour without the harshness of their larger cousins. They are usually sold near or around garlic and onions, are orange, reddish or slightly purple in colour and are almost completely round. Shallots can be substituted for red or Spanish onions. Use and store them as you would onions.

BIRD'S EYE CHILLIES

Thai chilli pepper, Prik khee noo

Said to be the hottest chilli in the world, bird's eye chillies are small red or green chilli peppers that pack a fiery punch and whose heat is not dissipated with cooking. Fresh chillies can keep for up to three weeks if stored in a plastic bag in the refrigerator. They might start wrinkling a little after five days, but are still usable as long as they are not bruised and deteriorating. Milder Mexican habanero chillies may be substituted for bird's eye chillies.

LEMONGRASS

Citronella, Heung mau, Sa, Tak rai, Sikai, Culs lakray, Sereh, Tanglad

This highly fragrant herb is sold in bundles of four or five and can usually be kept for about 10 days. They are long, dry-looking stalks, beige to pale green in colour and are about a foot in length. However, only 5 to 8 cm (2 to 3 in) of the bulb end are used because that part produces the most aroma. When using, cut off the tough root end and peel away the grass-like dry ends and outermost layers until you reveal a tender shoot with a light pink ring. When using, either chop finely or smash with a cleaver to release the fragrance. Choose stalks with large bulbous ends. If lemongrass is hard to come by, you can substitute the zest of half a lemon for one stalk of lemongrass.

CHINESE CHIVES

Gau choy, Nira

Although chives are used as herbs in western cooking, in the east they are used as a vegetable. These flat-bladed chives have an onion-garlic flavour and are at their best when of a dark green hue, free from blemishes or bruises. Regular chives can be substituted but with a slight alteration to the texture and taste. Flowering chives and yellow chives are similar in taste to Chinese chives, though again their texture is different, being more delicate. Chinese chives do not keep well at all so they are best used as soon as possible.

ROOT GINGER

The aromatic, pale yellow ginger plant is an important ingredient of Asian cooking and is an excellent source of vitamin C. When buying choose firm, swollen tubers with unwrinkled, shiny skins. Before using, the skin must be removed so that the juicy root can be grated, crushed, chopped, or sliced. Store root ginger in a cool, dry place for up to four weeks.

ERYNGO

Sawtooth herb, Saw leaf herb, Long cilantro, Cullantro, Ngo gai, Pak chi farang, Jii banal, Ketumbar jawa

A long, fresh, green leaf with serrated edges, eryngo is generally used as a last minute flavouring in soups and has a pleasant, cilantro-like taste. Used widely in Laos, Cambodia, Thailand and Vietnam, eryngo may be served raw, but is most often found in cooked dishes to offset strong flavours such as offal or innards. As with any leafy vegetable, choose fresh looking leaves without blemishes. It will keep for a few days in the refrigerator.

BASIL

Holy basil, Bai horapha, Thai basil, Bai gaprow

Unlike the sweet basil used in Italian cooking, Thai basil has little taste or smell when raw, but when cooked the flavours intensify and release a sharp anise taste. Thai basil stands up to heat much better than sweet basil, holding its own in curries, stews and soups. This herb has medium to dark green pointed leaves with purple flowers. Holy basil, or horapha basil has a spicier flavour and is also used to flavour curries and soups. Basil will keep for about four to five days in the refrigerator before starting to brown and wilt. Some varieties may even start browning after two to three days, so use it as soon as possible.

FLOWERING CHIVES

Garlic chives, Gau choy fa

A perennial plant that develops a strong root rather than a bulb. It has a mild garlic taste and may be used in place of common chives. Garlic chives can be cooked with or without their flower buds and can be eaten raw or cooked. Choose firm, green stalks with no visible bruising or wilting. Chives with unopened flower buds are more tender than those whose buds have flowered. When using, trim off a little of the bottom, as this part tends to be very tough. If left dry, flowering chives will keep for two to three days wrapped in kitchen paper, and in a plastic bag, in the refrigerator. Once the stems become even slightly bruised, the chives should be consumed immediately as they will deteriorate very quickly.

FRUIT VEGETABLES

BITTER MELON
Bitter gourd, Karela, Balsam pear, Fu gua

A staple throughout most of Asia, these fruits vary in shape, size, colour, texture and degree of bitterness. The ones found on the market are green and specifically picked when they are young for their bitterness. Ripe bitter melons are yellow to reddish-orange and are sometimes used in curries or pickling. In India, it is served at the beginning of the meal, either alone or with lentils and potato, while in China it is stir fried with a little black bean sauce sometimes with a little beef tossed in. It is high in potassium and dietary fibre but low in carbohydrates. It is also unsuitable for eating raw and blanching before cooking is highly recommended. You can also salt a bitter melon as you would an eggplant (aubergine) before cooking, to eliminate some of the bitterness. Keep refrigerated in your vegetable crisper for no more than five days.

FUZZY MELON
Hairy cucumber, Chinese wax gourd, Winter gourd, Tseet gua, Mo gua

A relative of the large winter melon, fuzzy melon comes in different shapes from spherical to elongated. Its colours vary from dark green to light greenish-yellow and it can be eaten young or mature. It should be peeled before cooking and can be cooked in any way as it takes on the flavours of the other ingredients. Upo and chayote make suitable substitutes in both taste and texture. Fuzzy melon keeps well in the lower part of your refrigerator often for up to two weeks.

EGGPLANT
Aubergine, Brinjal, Ai gua, Keh tzee, Terong

Unlike the normal eggplant (aubergine), Chinese eggplants are thin and long, with pale purplish hues rather than the dark, almost black, complexion of their western counterpart. The Japanese eggplant resembles the western eggplant but is shorter, while the Thai eggplant (*ma kheua pro*) is round, about the size of a ping pong ball with a green cap. It is white with light green markings or, less commonly, yellow-orange or purple in colour. The pea eggplant (*makheau phuang*) used in Thai cooking is actually not an eggplant at all. They are green, pea-sized, and grow in bunches. Usually added to Thai curries at the end of cooking, they have a slight bitter taste to them. Look for bright and shiny eggplants without dull skin. They will keep in the salad drawer for up to two weeks if they are bought fresh.

ANGLED LOOFAH
Ridged loofah, Silk gourd, Chinese okra, See gua

Although similar to a cucumber, the angled loofah is a far less attractive squash with ten sharp ridges and dull rough skin. Despite its appearance, it is very tasty when eaten raw or cooked. It holds up well when cooked for a short or extended period of time making it a perfect candidate for stir-fries or braised dishes. Only the young fruit is used in cooking as the mature fruit is very bitter and fibrous. Generally the skin is peeled but if you find a very young loofah, you could eat it skin and all. Choose firm, small-sized loofahs without any dark spots. Use as you would courgettes.

CHAYOTE
Choko, Fut sau gua, Vegetable pear, Christophine, Mirliton

A starchy fruit resembling the clasped hands of Buddha, fut sau gua means 'Buddha's hands melon.' Buy small, pale chayote so that the skin is edible, otherwise peel the skin. Many cookbooks suggest that its seed can also be eaten, but I do not recommend this. Scoop out the single seed and discard. You can use chayote raw in place of cucumber and it is also good stuffed and baked. Many cookbooks suggest that courgettes are a good substitute but I find that summer squash, bottle gourd and fuzzy melon are far better alternatives.

WINTER MELON
Dong gua

Although it looks like watermelon, and it is named a melon, it is actually a squash. The winter melon has dark green skin, which is occasionally mottled, with snow-white flesh and seeds. It has little taste of its own and generally takes on the flavours of the foods it is cooked with. For this reason it is good in soups or stews. Rinse and peel off the tough skin with a sharp knife. A famous Chinese dish, dong gua jung, uses a hollowed out winter melon as a tureen for a soup with chunks of melon swimming in the broth. It is also used as a filling for a Chinese pastry. A freshly sliced piece of melon will keep for about a week in the refrigerator if wrapped tightly in clingfilm.

KABOCHA

Winter squash, Nam gua, Fak thong

Kabocha is a round, slightly flattened, pumpkin-like squash with green, yellow or red skin. It tastes like pumpkin but is firmer in texture with less moisture. It is tender, sweet and extremely flavoursome. You can substitute it with regular pumpkin or any of the squashes such as butternut. Store and use as you would pumpkin. It generally keeps well and if cut open will keep for up to a week wrapped in clingfilm and stored in the refrigerator.

BOTTLE GOURD

Upo, Opo, Nam tao, Po gua, Woo lo gua, Lokhi, Cucuzzi

There are two types of bottle gourds, one shaped like a small baseball bat and the other a bottle. Only the young fruit is eaten and can be used in soups, braised, stir-fried or baked. It has a smooth, light green exterior and a mild tasting flesh similar to summer squash. When using, peel the skin and discard the spongy parts and seeds. When buying look for firm gourds with a shiny skin. They keep well and will last for three to four weeks if bought fresh. Winter melon, chayote and fuzzy melon are all good substitutes.

TUBERS

DAIKON
Lo bak

This tuber comes in different sizes. It can be short and round, long and thin or medium-sized. Generally, daikon is white with green stems, or the winter variety is green. Both can be substituted by kohlrabi if eaten cooked or by the common red radish if eaten raw. A fundamental item in Japanese cooking, daikon is used both raw and cooked, while in China daikon is almost always eaten cooked. It is also used with napa cabbage in Korean kimchee. Remove the skin with a peeler before cutting or grating. If grating, use within the hour as it will become soggy the longer it is left out. It is a highly perishable vegetable and when eaten raw, has a high potassium and vitamin C content. Unlike other root vegetables, daikon is not starchy or heavy. Choose daikon with firm, supple skins and store for up to two weeks in the refrigerator. A suitable substitute for daikon is icicle radish.

JICAMA
Yam bean, Saa gok

A slightly sweet vegetable resembling a giant turnip, this tuber has a leathery, pale tan skin and is an uneven round shape. Dried out jicama (pronounced 'hicama') can be spongy with a fibrous texture. With a sharp paring knife peel the skin leaving only the white flesh. At its prime, jicama should be crunchy, slightly fibrous, and moist with a slightly sweet taste and can be eaten raw in salads. It is less sweet than water chestnuts, but makes a reasonable substitute. When choosing jicama, make sure they are small, firm and have well-rounded roots without blemishes or mold. Feel its weight when selecting, as it should feel heavy for its size. Jicama will generally last about four to five days in the refrigerator, if bought fresh.

BURDOCK
Gobo

Although burdock is used in China as a herbal medicine, in Japan it is an important staple food. A slender, hairy taproot with a neutral taste, burdock must be soaked to remove its bitterness. When selecting burdock choose thin, long roots about 30 cm (1 foot) in length. Burdock can withstand extended cooking so it is best used in stews or slow simmering dishes, however, it can also be eaten raw. It will keep for a few days in the refrigerator, or longer if the soil is not removed when storing.

WATER CHESTNUTS
Ma tai

A marsh plant, fresh water chestnuts are edible tubers with pointed tops about three quarters of the size of a ping pong ball. They are sold unpeeled with soil or mud clinging to them. Underneath its shiny tough skin is sweet, slightly starchy and very crunchy white flesh. They are excellent in salads or stir-fried with other vegetables. When selecting, make sure they are free of wrinkles and mould. They keep well and will usually last up to two weeks in the refrigerator with the soil intact.

KOHLRABI
Gant-gobi, Gai lan tau, Choy tau guo

Although kohlrabi looks like a root, it is a thickened stem from the cabbage family. Pale green in colour with a round base, it is about the size of an orange often with spiky stems protruding from its top. Kohlrabi tastes similar to radish, can be eaten raw or cooked and is an excellent substitute for turnip, swede, or celeriac but with a more delicate, sweeter taste than turnip. Choose firm medium-sized roots that feel heavy for their size. To utilize it in the best way, peel after cooking when steaming or boiling. In all other types of cooking, peel before using. It will keep for four to five days in the refrigerator.

LOTUS ROOT
Leen ngau

A very porous rhizome, resembling sausage links in appearance, and adding a fibrous touch to soups, salads and braised dishes. Grown in ponds or flooded fields, it is also delicious steamed or stir-fried. When using, wash the root thoroughly, cut off the ends and peel the outer skin with a peeler. It can be substituted with potato or yam. Look for firm roots with as little bruising as possible. The root should be thick with small holes and once you cut the lotus root open it will quickly discolour, so soak it in a mixture of water and a splash of vinegar for 20 minutes, to help retain its colour. Lotus root does not keep well so use it as soon as you buy it.

ARROWHEAD

Tzee goo

Arrowheads are the size of water chestnuts and are crunchy in texture. When using peel and remove any visible sprouts and discard any arrowheads that feel limp when gently squeezed. Choose firm tubers with as little browning as possible. When fresh they are a creamy beige colour. Arrowheads are excellent in curries to give added texture and they are also wonderful sliced paper-thin and fried as an alternative to potato chips. Otherwise, use as you would jicama and water chestnuts. Arrowheads will keep for two to three days in the refrigerator.

BAMBOO SHOOTS

Bamboo shoots are considered a delicacy in Asia. Fresh shoots are covered with slender but sharp hairs, which must be removed before blanching. When raw they contain toxic substances that are destroyed on heating. Most people are familiar with the tinned variety but if you come across fresh bamboo shoots, give them a try as the canned variety are a far cry from the fresh. Like corn, one can only see if the shoots are fresh when the 'husks' are removed. Cut the tip of the shoot with a sharp knife and then slit it lengthways and remove the outer layer. The base can be discarded as only the tender 'shoot' is used. Boil it for 15 minutes before use. When fresh, they can be kept for up to five days in water provided that you rinse them and replace the water every day. Bamboo shoots can be added to braised dishes, stir fries and soups.

BEANS, FRUITS, AND SEAWEEDS

POMELO
Look yau, Shaddock

Pomelo is a thick skinned citrus resembling a large grapefruit. Peel away the thick layer of pith to reveal pulpy, sweet or tart flesh slightly milder in taste than grapefruit. It is also less juicy than grapefruit and can be either sweet or acidic. Pomelos are eaten as fruit in Asia just like grapefruit are in the West, but not predominantly for breakfast. When choosing, look for fruits that are heavy for their size, free of blemishes and sweetly fragrant. They can be stored in the refrigerator for up to a week.

LONG BEANS
Yard beans, Dau gok

These beans are actually long-pod cowpeas, so named because they grow up to one yard long. They resemble a bunch of shoelaces and are often sold curled into a coil. Mostly grey to greyish green pods, they are crunchy and when split down the middle reveal up to 30 edible seeds. Look for fresh, plump beans with a crisp snap. You can substitute with western string beans although their texture is slightly less crunchy. Long beans are wonderful blanched and tossed into a salad. Store in a plastic bag in the refrigerator for up to five days.

WAKAME
Seaweed

A type of seaweed from the brown algae family, wakame is sold dried or salted, usually in Japanese grocery stores. Any type of seaweed contains a high level of nutrients and minerals such as niacin, and wakame is no exception. When buying wakame in its salted form it should be dark green in colour while the dried variety looks something like light brown ribbons. When using dried wakame, rinse under the tap and soak in warm water until it becomes pliable. In Japan, wakame is added to soups or eaten blanched and tossed with dressing as a salad. In China, a form of wakame called black moss is used in a vegetarian dish called lo hon jai, which is eaten during Chinese New Year. It looks like hard brittle hair or a black scouring pad. Black moss must also be soaked in warm water before using.

EDAMAME

Mo dau, Fresh soybean

These green pods are grown to eat fresh as they are wonderfully tender and extremely flavousome. Generally sold fresh in Asia, in the west they are sold frozen section either shelled or enclosed in furry pods. An excellent source of protein, edamame should not be eaten raw as they contain a trypsin inhibitor. They are also hard to shell when raw so blanch them in some salted water before shelling and cooking them. Use in salads or just as a snack as one would with peanuts in the west.

TAMARIND

Mak kham, Sampolok

The fibrous, sticky ripe pod of this plant is highly valued for its sour fruit pulp used to flavour many Asian dishes. Widely used in Filipino and Thai cuisines as an addition to soups, its pulp must be mashed in water, then pressed through a sieve. Most Asian grocery stores carry a powdered form, which I prefer, making it easier to use and store. The powdered version is a lot more powerful and, therefore, should only be used sparingly, as you would use dried herbs compared to fresh ones.

KOMBU

Kelp, Seatangle, Hoi dai

In Japan, kombu is used to make the base of a broth known as dashi. It is generally sold in dried sheets with a whitish hue. This is a mould fundamental in making dashi. When using, cut off what you need and wipe with kitchen paper or a dry cloth. Do not wash, rinse or wipe with a damp cloth to remove the mould as by doing this you will be extracting the flavours, which should be going into your dashi. Japanese stores stock kombu in packets or Chinese shops will sell it in a jar. Store in a cool, dry place for up to six months.

STARFRUIT

Carambola, Yeung toe, Balimbing

There are two versions of this juicy fruit: green which are tart and yellow which are sweet. They have a wax-like skin, often green or pale yellow, turning golden yellow when ripe and they are easily recognizable by their five ridges. When cut open the slices resemble a star, hence its name. Starfruit can be eaten raw as a fruit or in salads, or can be excellent in cooked dishes such as curries, but it does not cook well, so it is generally added at the last minute. It often replaces mango in Indian chutney.

SIDE DISHES, SOUPS AND SALADS

WILTED MIZUNA WITH WALNUTS

MIZUNA IS A WONDERFUL RAW INGREDIENT IN SALADS. BUT I HAVE FOUND THAT WILTING IT SLIGHTLY WITH A DRESSING MAKES FOR A DELECTABLE VARIATION. I'VE ALSO THROWN IN SOME RED CABBAGE AND GREEN BEANS FOR COLOUR. USE YOUR IMAGINATION AND ZEST IT UP WITH A HANDFUL OF YELLOW AND RED PEPPERS FOR ADDED MEASURE.

INGREDIENTS

Serves 4

Preparation time: 20 minutes

Cooking time: 5 minutes

1 tbsp vegetable or sunflower oil

1 red onion, sliced

3 cloves garlic, peeled and crushed

120 g/4 oz green beans, julienned

120 g/4 oz red cabbage, julienned

120 g/4 oz mizuna, chopped coarsely

3 tbsp rice vinegar

50 g/2 oz walnuts, chopped

METHOD

1   Heat the oil in a pan on a medium high heat and sauté the onion and garlic for 1 minute.

2   Add the green beans and sauté for 1 minute or until the colour becomes darker.

3   Add the red cabbage and sauté for a further minute.

4   Add the mizuna and sauté for another minute. Stir in the vinegar and remove from the heat.

5   Combine the vegetables with the walnuts and serve immediately.

GREEN PAPAYA SEAFOOD SALAD
WITH CITRUS SOY DRESSING

MANY SEAFOOD SALADS ARE LADEN WITH MAYONNAISE BUT I FIND SEAFOOD IS BEST WHEN COMBINED WITH A TART PARTNER. SO HERE I'VE USED GREEN PAPAYA AND UTILIZED ITS NATURALLY SOUR TASTE AS A PERFECT COMPLEMENT TO THE PRAWNS, CRAB, AND CALAMARI.

INGREDIENTS

Serves 2 as a main dish
  or 4 as a side dish

Preparation time: 30 minutes

Cooking time: 8 minutes

10 large prawns, uncooked, with shells

120 g/4 oz uncooked calamari

120 g/4 oz cooked crabmeat

1 medium green papaya, shredded or julienned

1 tbsp coriander or parsley leaves, chopped, to garnish

For the Dressing

2 cloves garlic, crushed

4 tbsp light soy sauce

1 tbsp lemon juice

1 tbsp lime juice

1½ tbsp sugar

METHOD

1   Blanch the prawns and calamari by covering them with boiling water. Remove the calamari after 2 minutes or it will become tough, but leave the prawns for 2 minutes more. Then plunge both into icy water.

2   When chilled, peel and devein the prawns and cut halfway across the body lengthways and halfway across widthways. Cut the calamari into small pieces equal to the size of the prawns. Mix together the prawns, calamari, and cooked crabmeat.

3   Arrange the papaya strips loosely and place the seafood around them.

4   In a jar or bowl mix together the ingredients for the dressing. Drizzle the dressing on to the papaya and seafood, sprinkle with chopped coriander and serve.

QUICK ASIAN GREENS SOUP

THIS IS A FAST LUNCH I OFTEN MAKE WHEN PRESSED FOR TIME. IT IS LIGHT AND GOES WELL WITH A BOWL OF STEAMED RICE OR SOME HOT CRUSTY BREAD.

INGREDIENTS

Serves 1
Preparation time: 5 minutes
Cooking time: 6 to 8 minutes

400g/14 oz carton chicken stock

4 napa cabbage leaves, julienned

1 stalk baby bok choy or Shanghai
  bok choy

½ tsp sesame oil

Salt to taste, if necessary

White pepper

METHOD

1   In a pan, bring the chicken stock to the boil.

2   Add the napa cabbage, bring to the boil then simmer for 3 to 4 minutes.

3   Add the bok choy and simmer for a further 2 to 3 minutes or until tender.

4   Remove from the heat, stir in the sesame oil and salt, if required, and a dash of pepper. Serve piping hot.

GINGER JUICE

FRESH GINGER JUICE IMPARTS A REFRESHING, CITRUS-LIKE AROMA AND FLAVOUR TO YOUR DISHES. THE FRESHER THE EXTRACTED JUICE, THE BETTER THE FLAVOUR OF YOUR DISH.

INGREDIENTS

Makes 4-6 tablespoons
Preparation time 10 minutes

10 cm/4-in piece of root ginger, peeled and cut into 2.5 cm/1 in chunks

15 x 15 cm/6 x 6 in piece muslin

METHOD

1 Place the root ginger chunks into a food processor and mince.

2 Squeeze the chopped root ginger through muslin to extract the juice and use immediately.

WINTER MELON CRABMEAT SOUP

WINTER MELON ADAPTS WELL TO SO MANY INGREDIENTS BECAUSE OF ITS MILD FLAVOUR. WHEN ENTERTAINING, I LIKE TO ADD A HANDFUL OF DICED CARROTS TO GIVE IT A BURST OF COLOUR.

INGREDIENTS

Serves 4
Preparation time: 25 minutes
Cooking time: 20 minutes

1 l/1$\frac{3}{4}$ pt chicken stock

4 dried or fresh shiitake mushrooms, soaked and diced

1 tbsp rice vinegar

450 g/1 lb winter melon, peeled and diced

5 tbsp cooked crabmeat

1 tbsp chopped coriander

White pepper

METHOD

1 Bring the chicken stock to the boil in a large pan. Add the mushrooms and rice vinegar and simmer for 5 minutes.

2 Add the melon and simmer for 10 minutes or until tender.

3 Add the crabmeat and remove from the heat.

4 Stir in the coriander and a dash of pepper. Serve immediately.

MIXED VEGETABLES
WITH PEANUT SAUCE

FOR THIS INDONESIAN SIGNATURE DISH. I LIKE TO USE ALL SORTS OF VEGETABLES. AS LONG AS THEY ARE MILD IN FLAVOUR AND RETAIN THEIR FIRMNESS AFTER COOKING. IF YOU USE SWEET PEANUT BUTTER. OMIT THE KECAP MANIS AND ADD ONE TEASPOON OF DARK SOY SAUCE INSTEAD.

INGREDIENTS

Serves 4

Preparation time: 20 minutes

Cooking time: 35 minutes

120 g/4 oz long beans, cut into
 2.5 cm/1 in lengths

120 g/4 oz cabbage, shredded

175 g/6 oz bean sprouts

120g/4 oz napa cabbage, cut into
 2.5 cm/1 in squares

4 pieces fried firm tofu (bean curd),
 cut into 1 cm/$^1/_2$ in strips

3 eggs, hard-boiled and quartered

Chilli oil, to serve

For the peanut sauce

5 tbsp crunchy peanut butter

225 ml/8 fl oz coconut milk

2 tsp sambal oelek (see page 47)

2 tsp kecap manis (see page 48)
 or 1 tsp dark soy sauce and 2 tsp sugar

Chilli flakes, plus extra to garnish

METHOD

1   Blanch the vegetables by covering them in boiling water for about 3 to 5 minutes. Remove and immediately plunge them into icy cold water to retain their colour and firmness.

2   Use a medium size non-stick pan for the sauce. Over a medium heat, melt the peanut butter with the coconut milk, stirring continuously to keep the mixture from burning.

3   Add the remaining sauce ingredients stirring all the time on a low heat until thoroughly mixed and the sauce has a thickish consistency.

4   Divide the vegetables and tofu (bean curd) between four plates, place the egg quarters on top and pour over the sauce. Sprinkle with more chilli flakes, if desired.

LEMONGRASS-INFUSED
COCONUT SOUP

ON COLD NIGHTS I FIND MYSELF LONGING FOR THE COMFORTING WARMTH OF SOME HOT SOUP. THE HEAT FROM THE CHILLIES GIVES IT AN ADDED PUNCH. IF YOUR TOLERANCE OF CHILLIES IS MINIMAL, HALVE THE AMOUNT OF BIRD'S EYE CHILLIES. THIS SOUP WILL KEEP IN THE REFRIGERATOR FOR UP TO TWO DAYS OR IN THE FREEZER FOR UP TO A MONTH.

INGREDIENTS

Serves 4

Preparation time: 35 minutes

Cooking time: 20 minutes

1.7 l/3 pts chicken stock

4 chicken breasts, boneless, skinless

3 stalks lemongrass, sliced thinly
  (use the hearts only)

120 g/4 oz galangal, sliced thinly

120 g/4 oz enoki mushrooms

2 shallots, sliced thinly

3 kaffir lime leaves, torn

large bunch coriander, chopped coarsely

1 tbsp bird's eye chillies, chopped

4 tbsp fish sauce

3 tbsp lime juice

1 tsp sugar

4 tbsp coconut milk

2 tsp salt (if using home-made stock)

METHOD

1. In a pan, bring the stock to the boil. Add chicken breasts and poach for about 3 to 5 minutes. Remove the chicken breasts from the stock, cut into cubes and set aside.
Put all the remaining ingredients into the stock and boil for about 10 minutes.

2. Add the chicken to the stock and turn the heat low, simmering for about 3 minutes. Remove the lime leaves and galangal pieces before serving.

SQUASH COCONUT SOUP

MY JAPANESE AUNT MAKES WONDERFUL DISHES FROM KABOCHA SQUASH. ONE OF WHICH IS A STEW-LIKE DISH ALMOST LIKE A SOUP. ONE DAY I TRIED ADDING SOME LEFTOVER COCONUT MILK AND BOK CHOY IN THE REFRIGERATOR. I THREW THEM INTO THE PAN ALONGSIDE THE SQUASH. AND I WAS PLEASED TO FIND IT TURNED OUT SURPRISINGLY WELL!

INGREDIENTS

Serves 4

Preparation time: 20 minutes

Cooking time: 30 minutes

1.1 l/2 pts vegetable stock

175 g/6 oz squash (kabocha, acorn, or butternut), peeled, seeded and cut into bite-sized pieces

225 ml/8 fl oz coconut milk

2 shallots, grilled

1 tsp salt

$\frac{1}{4}$ tsp white pepper

1 large stalk bok choy, cut into bite-sized pieces

3 spring onions, chopped finely

METHOD

1 In a large pan, heat the stock and add the squash, and stir occasionally until the stock comes to a complete boil.

2 Reduce the heat, add the coconut milk, shallots, salt and pepper. Return to the boil and then reduce the heat, and simmer for about 15 minutes until the squash is tender.

3 Add the bok choy, stir for 1 minute, then remove from the heat.

4 Serve sprinkled with the spring onions.

FOUR SEASONS CITRUS SALAD

I NEVER HAD A TASTE FOR POMELO AS A CHILD. BUT YEARS LATER
I WAS WALKING IN THE STREETS OF CHINATOWN AND SAW A PILE
OF POMELOS SITTING NEATLY STACKED IN ROWS. AT THE TIME I
WAS PREGNANT AND AN OVERWHELMING CRAVING CAME OVER ME.
I IMMEDIATELY BOUGHT TWO POMELOS AND THIS RECIPE IS A
RESULT OF MY EXPERIMENTATION!

INGREDIENTS

Serves 4

Preparation time: 30 minutes

Cooking time: 5 minutes

1 blood (or any other seasonal) orange

1 tangerine or mandarin orange

1 pink grapefruit

1 pomelo

Vegetable oil for frying

**1 shallot, peeled and sliced
thinly, for garnish**

Shredded mint leaves, to garnish

For the dressing

2 tbsp lime juice

2 tbsp lemon juice

1 tbsp fish sauce

1 tsp sugar

½ tsp chilli flakes (optional)

Remaining juice from the fruit

METHOD

1   Peel the citrus fruits using a paring knife to remove the pith. Break up the fruit into
    small pieces and place in a bowl big enough to toss.

2   Drain the juice from the fruits and set aside.

3   In a bowl or jar, mix together the dressing ingredients including the remaining juice
    from the fruit.

4   Toss the fruit and dressing together.

5   Using a small pan, heat the oil over a medium high heat and fry the shallots until evenly
    brown, about 3 to 5 minutes. Drain on kitchen paper. Serve the salad in individual bowls
    with a sprinkle of shredded mint leaves, fried shallots and toasted sesame seeds.

GREEN BEANS WITH WAKAME

ALTHOUGH HERE IT IS SERVED WARM. THIS RECIPE IS EXTREMELY VERSATILE AND CAN BE PREPARED AHEAD OF TIME AND SERVED CHILLED. WARM OR AT ROOM TEMPERATURE.

INGREDIENTS

*Serves 2 as a main dish
 or 4 as a side dish
Preparation time: 5 minutes
Cooking time: 10 minutes*

500 g/1 lb green beans, trimmed

1 tbsp olive oil

1 kg/2 lb wakame, soaked
 and sliced thinly

1 tsp sesame seeds, to garnish

1 tsp soy sauce

METHOD

1. Blanch the green beans by covering them in boiling water for 1 minute. Remove and plunge them into icy cold water to retain their colour and firmness.

2. Heat a pan until hot and allow the beans to dry cook for 2 to 3 minutes. When the greens begin to shrivel add the oil and wakame and toss for 2 to 3 minutes.

3. Add the soy sauce and remove from the heat. Garnish with sesame seeds and serve.

SIMPLE THAI CURRY PASTE

IF YOU ARE NOT ABLE TO FIND THAI CURRY PASTE. YOU CAN MAKE A SIMPLE ONE YOURSELF. THAI CURRY PASTE FORMS THE BASIS OF AROMATIC CURRIES WITH CHICKEN. VEGETABLES. OR FISH.

INGREDIENTS

*Makes 1 serving
Preparation time: 15 minutes*

8 Thai chillies

3 shallots, chopped

1 tbsp coriander, chopped

2 kaffir lime leaves, chopped

2 stalks lemongrass, chopped
 (use only hearts)

1 tbsp shrimp paste

1 tbsp galangal (or root ginger),
 peeled and chopped

2 cloves garlic, peeled
 and chopped

$\frac{1}{4}$ tsp salt

METHOD

Combine all the ingredients in a food processor or crush and blend with a mortar and pestle until a smooth paste forms. Store in the refrigerator for no more than 3 days.

CHILLI DIPPING SAUCE

THIS BEAUTIFULLY SIMPLE RECIPE IS ONE OF THE BASICS OF ASIAN CUISINE AND CAN BE USED TO COMPLEMENT A HOST OF DISHES FROM DEEP FRIED TEMPURA-STYLE VEGETABLES TO THAI FISH CAKES OR CHICKEN.

INGREDIENTS

Makes 450 ml/16 fl oz	120 ml/4 fl oz fish sauce	2 tsp sambal oelek
Preparation time :5 minutes	450 ml/16 fl oz water	(see page 47)
Cooking time: 5 minutes	175 g/6 oz sugar	

METHOD

1. Mix together all the ingredients and heat in a saucepan. Bring to the boil and simmer for 3 minutes.

2. Chill in the refrigerator before using.

FRAGRANT RELISH

MAINLY, I SERVE THIS RELISH WITH SPICY FOODS TO COUNTERACT STRONGLY SPICED DISHES. IT CAN BE USED AS A DIP FOR CORNCHIPS, WITH CRUDITES AND ON BAKED POTATOES.

INGREDIENTS

Makes 225 ml/8 fl oz	1-2 green chillies, seeded and chopped	6 tbsp mint leaves
Preparation time: 30 minutes		6 tbsp coriander
	1 large garlic clove, peeled and crushed	Freshly ground black pepper
1-2 tbsp lemon or lime juice		225 ml/8 fl oz natural yoghurt
1 spring onion, chopped finely	$\frac{1}{2}$-1 tsp ground cumin	
	$\frac{1}{2}$ tsp sugar	

METHOD

1. Place all the ingredients except the yogurt into a blender or food processor and blend until smooth.

2. Stir in the yoghurt. Add more lemon juice, sugar and black pepper if desired.

3. The relish is best used immediately, or within 2 hours. The longer you keep it the less fragrant it becomes.

DAIKON SALAD

SERVED AS A STARTER, THE TANGY, PIQUANT FLAVOURS OF THIS SALAD STIMULATE THE SENSES AND WHET THE APPETITE. YOU CAN·TRY A VARIATION OF THIS DISH USING GREEN DAIKON, GREEN MANGO, OR GREEN PAPAYA, OR A COMBINATION OF ALL OF THEM!

INGREDIENTS

Serves 2

Preparation time: 15 minutes

Cooking time: 5 minutes

7-8 long beans, cut into
 2.5 cm/1 in lengths

300 g/10 oz daikon, julienned

7-8 cherry tomatoes, halved

6 tbsp dried shrimps,
 softened in boiling water

1 clove garlic, peeled and chopped

1 bird's eye chilli, chopped,
 or crushed chilli flakes

1½ tbsp lemon juice

1½ tbsp fish sauce

1 tbsp brown sugar

1 tbsp crushed peanuts,
 to serve (optional)

METHOD

1   Blanch the long beans by covering them in slightly salted boiling water then plunging them into icy cold water to retain their colour and firmness. Drain and allow to cool.

2   In a bowl, combine the daikon, beans and tomatoes, then set aside.

3   In a mortar and pestle or food processor, mix together the dried shrimps, garlic, chilli, lemon juice, fish sauce, and brown sugar.

4   Combine the daikon mixture and the vegetables and mix and toss until the vegetables 'wilt' and soften.

5   Serve topped with crushed peanuts.

WILTED AMARANTH
IN PINE NUT DRESSING

YOU CAN USE RED- OR GREEN-VEINED AMARANTH FOR THIS RECIPE.
SPINACH WORKS JUST AS WELL IF AMARANTH IS HARD TO FIND.

INGREDIENTS

Serves 4

Preparation time: 30 minutes

Cooking time: 20 minutes

**1 kg/2 lbs amaranth leaves, tough
stems discarded**

For the dressing

75 g/3 oz pine nuts, toasted and lightly crushed

3 tbsp dark soy sauce

METHOD

1 Blanch the amaranth leaves by covering them in boiling water for 1 minute. Remove
and immediately plunge them into icy water. Drain thoroughly and squeeze any
excess water out. Chill the leaves in the refrigerator for at least 10 minutes.

2 Mix the pine nuts and soy sauce in a bowl to make the dressing. Toss with the
leaves before serving.

ASIAN PESTO

WHEN I DON'T QUITE HAVE THE ENERGY TO MAKE A MEAL, I AM ALWAYS GRATEFUL TO HAVE THIS IN THE REFRIGERATOR. THROW SOME SALMON ON THE GRILL, SERVE WITH A GENEROUS DOLLOP OF PESTO AND CALL IT A NIGHT.

INGREDIENTS

Makes 225 ml/8 fl oz

Preparation time: 30 minutes

Cooking time: 5 minutes

Juice of 1 lime

1 cup Thai basil leaves

50 rau ram leaves

250 g/2 oz toasted unsalted peanuts, ground (optional)

1 small chilli, seeded and chopped

3 cloves garlic , peeled and crushed

1 tsp root ginger, peeled and shredded

5 tbsp vegetable or sunflower oil

METHOD

1 Mix together all the ingredients and heat in a saucepan. Bring to the boil and simmer for 3 minutes.

2 Chill in the refrigerator before using.

SAMBAL OELEK

THIS SUPER HOT SAUCE IS GREAT FOR ADDING TO RECIPES. USE IT SPARINGLY WITH FISH CAKES OR SPRING ROLLS.

INGREDIENTS

Makes 225 ml/8 fl oz

Preparation time: 15 minutes

Cooking time: 10 minutes

30 red chillies

2 cloves garlic, peeled

$\frac{1}{4}$ onion

2 tbsp sugar

2 tbsp lemon or lime juice

2-3 tbsp water

METHOD

1 Combine all the ingredients in a blender and blend until a smooth paste forms.

2 Transfer to a pan and cook for 10 minutes on a medium heat.

3 Cool and store in an airtight jar in the refrigerator for up to two weeks.

KECAP MANIS

THIS HOME-MADE VERSION OF SWEET SOY SAUCE IS SIMPLE TO MAKE
AND TASTES MUCH FRESHER THAN THE SHOP BOUGHT VARIETY.

INGREDIENTS

Makes 175 ml/6 fl oz

Preparation time: 10 minutes

Cooking time: 10 minutes

120 g/4 oz light brown sugar

175 ml/6 fl oz water

3 tbsp dark molasses

6 tbsp low sodium soy sauce

½ tsp ground coriander

¼ tsp freshly ground
  black pepper

METHOD

1 Combine the sugar, water, and molasses in a pan, bring to the boil and cook for about
5 minutes or until the ingredients have dissolved.

2 Stir in the remaining ingredients and simmer for about 4 to 5 minutes
stirring occasionally.

3 Cool and store in an airtight jar in the refrigerator for up to four days.

FRESH CORIANDER RELISH

WHIP UP A BOWL OF THIS REFRESHING RELISH AND HAVE A BARBECUE TO
REMEMBER. USE FISH SAUCE INSTEAD OF SALT AND OMIT THE GARAM
MASALA FOR A SOUTHEAST ASIAN TWIST.

INGREDIENTS

Makes 225 ml/8 fl oz
Preparation time: 20 minutes

120 g/4 oz coriander
6 spring onions, sliced finely

2 green chillies, seeded
  and chopped

5 tbsp lemon juice

1 tsp salt

2 tsp sugar

1 tsp garam masala
(or ⅓ tsp each of ground
coriander, cumin, and freshly
ground black pepper)

2 tbsp water

METHOD

1 In a blender or food processor, mix together the coriander, spring onions,
chillies and one tablespoon of the lemon juice for about 1 minute or until smooth.

2 Pour into a bowl and stir in the remaining ingredients. Best used on day of making.

2 | VEGETABLES
AND VEGETARIAN DISHES

WATER SPINACH WITH CHILLIES

ENJOYED ALL OVER SOUTHEAST ASIA. WATER SPINACH IS BEST WHEN STIR FRIED WITH SHRIMP PASTE AND A LITTLE CHILLI. YOU MAY WANT TO SUBSTITUTE SHRIMP PASTE FOR TOFU (BEAN CURD) OR MUSHROOM SOY WHICH WILL GIVE JUST AS MUCH FLAVOUR.

INGREDIENTS

Serves 4 as a side dish

Preparation time: 15 minutes

Cooking time: 10 minutes

$1\frac{1}{2}$ tbsp vegetable or sunflower oil

1 tbsp shallots, chopped

1 clove garlic, crushed

1 tbsp red chillies, seeded and chopped

$1\frac{1}{2}$ tbsp shrimp paste, or 1 tbsp fish sauce, or 3 tbsp mushroom soy

6 oz kangkung, cut into 5 cm/2 in pieces

$\frac{1}{2}$ tsp sugar

METHOD

1 Heat the oil in a pan and stir fry the shallots, garlic, and chillies for about 2 minutes or until light brown.

2 Add the shrimp paste and sugar and fry together for 1 to 2 minutes.

3 Add the kangkung and toss with the mixture quickly for about 3 minutes or until the kangkung starts to wilt. Should it get too dry, add a tablespoon of water and continue to toss until the kangkung is tender.

4 Remove from the heat and serve immediately with rice crackers or steamed rice.

ASIAN VEGETABLE STEW

A QUICK AND SIMPLE STEW ENJOYED STEAMING HOT OR AT ROOM
TEMPERATURE. THIS IS AN EXCELLENT ACCOMPANIMENT TO ANY
LIGHT MAIN COURSE SUCH AS FISH. IT IS ALSO EXCELLENT AS A
VEGETARIAN MAIN COURSE AND USUALLY GOES DOWN WELL
WHEN FRIENDS POP IN FOR A VISIT.

INGREDIENTS

*Serves 4 as a side dish
  or 2 as a main dish*

Preparation time: 10 minutes

Cooking time: 20 minutes

2 tbsp vegetable or sunflower oil

**1 eggplant (aubergine), cut into
  1 cm/½ inch cubes**

**6 okra pods, trimmed
  (do not pierce pods!)**

**120g/4 oz kabocha or butternut squash,
  cut into 1 cm/½ in cubes**

120 ml/4 fl oz vegetable stock

2 tbsp soy sauce

2 tbsp mirin

½ tsp salt

Pinch of freshly ground black pepper

½ tsp sugar

METHOD

1   In a medium-sized saucepan, heat one tablespoon of oil and fry the eggplant
    and okra for 2 to 3 minutes. Set aside.

2   Heat the remaining oil and fry the squash for 3 to 4 minutes.

3   Add the stock, soy sauce, mirin, salt, pepper, and sugar and simmer for 3 minutes.

4   Return the eggplant and okra to the pan and simmer for a further 3 to 4 minutes
    or until all the vegetables are tender.

STIR FRIED GAI LAN WITH ROOT GINGER

THE MUSTARDY TASTE OF GAI LAN CAN SOMETIMES BE VERY OVERPOWERING SO ADDING ROOT GINGER HELPS TO BALANCE OUT THE FLAVOURS. GAI LAN ALSO HAS A FRAGRANCY WHICH GIVES ANY DISH AN ADDED BOOST.

INGREDIENTS

Serves 4

Preparation time: 10 minutes

Cooking time: 5 to 7 minutes

3 tbsp fish sauce, or mushroom soy

3 tbsp water

2.5 cm/1 in piece root ginger, peeled and julienned

2 tbsp vegetable or sunflower oil

450 g/1 lb gai lan stalks and leaves, cut into large pieces

METHOD

1   Combine the fish sauce, water and root ginger and set aside.

2   Heat the oil in a pan or wok over a high heat. When hot, add the gai lan and stir fry for about 2 to 3 minutes or until the leaves are a little wilted.

3   Stir in the fish sauce mixture and fry for 2 to 3 minutes until well combined. Serve immediately.

FLOWERING CHIVES
WITH CARROT AND ONION

A WONDERFUL TRI-COLOURED DISH ESPECIALLY IMPRESSIVE WHEN ENTERTAINING. THE COMBINATION OF TEXTURES ALSO MAKES FOR AN EXCELLENT CONTRAST TO WHATEVER MEATS YOU ARE SERVING. IT IS LOW IN CALORIES AS NO OIL IS USED.

INGREDIENTS

Serves 4 as a side dish

Preparation time: 15 minutes

Cooking time: 10 minutes

175 g/6 oz flowering chives, cut into 2.5 cm/1 in lengths

1 onion, sliced thinly

90 g/3 oz carrots, julienned

2 tsp soy sauce

1 tbsp lemon juice

$\frac{1}{2}$ tsp sugar

2 tbsp toasted sesame seeds, to garnish

Lime wedges and rice crackers, to serve

METHOD

1 Blanch chives, onions and carrots separately by covering them with slightly salted boiling water then plunging them into icy cold water to retain their colour and texture.

2 Drain the excess water and leave them to cool.

3 Toss with soy sauce, lemon juice and sugar.

4 Sprinkle with sesame seeds, and serve cold with lime wedges and rice crackers.

CHOY SUM WITH LIME DRESSING

ONE OF THE MOST WIDELY USED VEGETABLES IN ASIA, CHOY SUM IS SO MILD TASTING THAT IT IS EASY TO USE IN VIRTUALLY ANY ASIAN RECIPE. THE ADDED TEXTURE OF FRIED GARLIC, CHILLI, AND SPRING ONIONS IS SIMPLY A BOLD ATTEMPT TO FLIRT WITH YOUR TASTEBUDS!

INGREDIENTS

Serves 4

Preparation time: 10 minutes

Cooking time: 5 minutes

2 tbsp vegetable or sunflower oil

3 fresh chillies, seeded and julienned

4 garlic cloves, peeled and sliced finely

6 spring onions, cut on the diagonal

450 g/1 lb choy sum

1 tbsp crushed peanuts

For the dressing

1-2 tbsp fish sauce, or mushroom soy

2 tbsp lime juice

225 ml/8 fl oz coconut milk

METHOD

1   In a frying pan, heat the oil and fry the chillies for 2 to 3 minutes. Remove with a slotted spoon onto kitchen paper to drain off any excess oil.

2   Add the garlic and fry for 1 minute or until golden brown. Remove and set aside on kitchen paper.

3   Add the spring onions and stir fry for 1 minute. Remove and set aside on kitchen paper .

4   Place the choy sum in a serving bowl and sprinkle with fried chilli, garlic, spring onions and peanuts.

5   In a separate jar or bowl, mix the dressing ingredients together. Pour the dressing over the vegetables and serve immediately.

CRISPY GREENS

THIS RECIPE IS TRADITIONALLY USED AS A BED FOR SPICY CHICKEN, BUT OVER THE YEARS SO MANY PEOPLE HAVE COMMENTED ON IT THAT I BELIEVE IT SHOULD RANK AS A SIDE DISH IN ITS OWN RIGHT. I HOPE YOU AGREE!

INGREDIENTS

Serves 4 as a side dish

Preparation time: 20 minutes

Cooking time: 20 minutes

300 g/10 oz green leaves (gai lan, bok choy)

$\frac{1}{4}$ **tsp salt**

2 tsp light brown sugar

Vegetable or sunflower oil for deep frying

3 tbsp whole roasted peanuts

METHOD

1   Shred the leaves and allow to air dry for at least two hours.
They should be completely dry when you are ready to use them.

2   Mix the salt and brown sugar together in a bowl and set aside.

3   Heat the oil in a deep pan at least 10 cm/4 inches high to about 190-200°C (375-400°F).

4   Fry the leaves a handful at a time for about 30 seconds, or until slightly darkened and shrivelled. Make sure they do not burn. Remove from the pan and drain on kitchen paper. Keep the leaves warm in a low oven (110°C/225°F/gas mark ¼)

5   When all the leaves have been fried, add the nuts and toss well.
Serve with the salt and sugar mixture on the side, for sprinkling.

TAJ MAHAL BEANS

I AM NO EXPERT WHEN IT COMES TO INDIAN FOOD, BUT THE FLAVOURS FROM THIS SPLENDID CULTURE INSPIRED ME TO CREATE THIS RECIPE. THE REGAL NATURE OF THE SPICES DRESS UP WHAT IS, ESSENTIALLY, A REALLY SIMPLE DISH.

INGREDIENTS

Serves 4

Preparation time: 5 minutes

Cooking time: 8 minutes

1 tbsp vegetable or sunflower oil

$1/4$ tsp turmeric

1-2 tsp garam masala (or $1/3$ tsp each of ground coriander, cumin and freshly ground black pepper)

450 g/1 lb long beans, cut into 2.5 cm/1 in lengths

1 tbsp fresh lemon juice

METHOD

1   Heat the oil in a non-stick pan, add the spices and stir for about 30 seconds.

2   Add the beans and fry over a high heat for 5 minutes or until the beans begin to wrinkle. Add the lemon juice, toss and serve.

SIMMERED AMARANTH WITH GARLIC

AS A LITTLE GIRL I LOVED MY MOTHER MAKING THIS DISH WITH THE STRIKING RED-VEINED AMARANTH. THE SAUCE WOULD HAVE A PINK HUE, WHICH CONTRASTED BEAUTIFULLY WITH THE SNOWY WHITE RICE THAT ACCOMPANIED IT.

INGREDIENTS

Serves 4

Preparation time: 15 minutes

Cooking time: 10 to 15 minutes

1 tbsp vegetable or sunflower oil

8 large cloves garlic, peeled

900 g/2 lb amaranth leaves, trimmed, tough stems discarded

225 ml/8 fl oz vegetable stock

1 tsp salt

METHOD

1 In a wok or large pan, heat the oil and fry the garlic cloves until browned.

2 Add the amaranth leaves and stir frequently until wilted, about 3 to 4 minutes, depending on the thickness of the stems.

3 Add the stock and bring to the boil, lower the heat and simmer for 4 to 5 minutes or until the leaves are softened.

4 Add the salt, stir and serve.

GREENS
WITH SESAME AND ROOT GINGER

THIS DISH COMBINES BABY BOK CHOY AND NAPA CABBAGE TO CREATE MIXED GREENS BUT USE WHATEVER IS AVAILABLE AND FRESH AT YOUR MARKET TO MAKE YOUR OWN VERSION. REMEMBER TO ADD VINEGAR AT THE VERY LAST MINUTE AS SIMMERING VEGETABLES WITH VINEGAR WILL ZAP THE COLOUR RIGHT OUT OF THEM.

INGREDIENTS

Serves 4

Preparation time: 20 minutes

Cooking time: 5 minutes

4 tbsp vegetable or sunflower oil

4 tsp fresh root ginger,
  peeled and chopped

2 cloves garlic, peeled and chopped

8 fresh shiitake mushrooms,
  cut in half with stems removed

225 g/8 oz napa cabbage,
  cut into bite-sized pieces

225 g/8 oz baby bok choy,
  cut into bite-sized pieces

2 tsp soy sauce

4 tsp rice vinegar

3 tbsp sesame seeds, to garnish

METHOD

1   Heat the oil in a wok or medium-sized frying pan and stir fry the root ginger and garlic for 1 minute or until the garlic starts to brown.

2   Add the mushrooms and napa cabbage, stir for 1 minute. Then add the baby bok choy, and one teaspoon of soy sauce. Cover for about 1 minute.

3   Add the remaining soy sauce and the vinegar and stir fry for another minute then remove from the heat.

4   Sprinkle with sesame seeds before serving.

STIR FRIED BOK CHOY
AND MUSHROOM

EVERY FAMILY HAS THEIR OWN WAY OF SERVING THIS VERSATILE DISH. IT IS ONE OF THE MOST COMMON WAYS IN WHICH TO SERVE GREENS. YOU CAN USE ANY CHINESE VEGETABLE SUCH AS SHANGHAI BOK CHOY, GAI LAN, OR CHOY SUM WITH ONE OR ALL THREE TYPES OF MUSHROOMS I HAVE LISTED.

INGREDIENTS

Serves 4

Preparation time: 10 minutes

Cooking time: 5 minutes

4 dried black Chinese mushrooms

1 tbsp vegetable or sunflower oil

1 clove garlic, peeled and crushed

450 g/1 lb bok choy, cut into bite-sized pieces

50 g/2 oz oyster mushrooms, rinsed, stems discarded

50 g/2 oz shiitake mushrooms, rinsed, stems discarded

2 tbsp oyster sauce

METHOD

1 Rinse the dried mushrooms thoroughly and then soak them in half a cup of boiling water or enough to completely cover the mushrooms. Let them stand for 30 minutes. Squeeze any excess water out of the mushrooms, then cut them in half and set the soaking liquid aside.

2 Heat the oil in a wok or frying pan and stir fry the garlic until light brown, about 2 minutes.

3 Add the bok choy and fry for 1 minute, then add the oyster and shiitake mushrooms and fry for 2 minutes more.

4 Stir in the soaking liquid and oyster sauce, toss quickly and serve.

SAUTÉED LONG BEANS

THERE ARE MANY VERSIONS OF SAUTÉED BEANS IN ASIA WHICH IS PROBABLY BECAUSE THEY GO WELL WITH SEAFOOD OR MEATS. THEY CAN BE ENJOYED ON THEIR OWN SAUTÉED IN GARLIC. THIS IS A MILD, NON-SPICY VERSION THAT IS AUTHENTIC AND VERSATILE ENOUGH TO ACCOMPANY MOST DISHES.

INGREDIENTS

Serves 4

Preparation time: 25 minutes

Cooking time: 10 minutes

2 tbsp vegetable or sunflower oil

1 clove garlic, peeled and crushed

1 onion, chopped

2 ripe tomatoes, diced

¼ tsp fish sauce or mushroom soy

Freshly ground black pepper

225 g/8 oz long beans,
   cut into 1 cm/½ in lengths

METHOD

1 In a frying pan, heat the oil and sauté the garlic and onion until golden brown.

2 Add the tomatoes and cook until soft, stir for 1 minute.

3 Stir in the fish sauce and pepper and bring to the boil. Add the long beans and cook for 2 to 3 minutes, stirring occasionally or until the beans are slightly tender but still crisp. Serve piping hot.

GARLIC A-CHOY

I FIRST TASTED A-CHOY IN TAIPEI WHEN I DINED AT A STREET STALL. NEEDLESS TO SAY, I IMMEDIATELY FELL IN LOVE WITH ITS CRISP, FRESH TEXTURE. I PREFER A-CHOY SLIGHTLY WILTED, THOUGH IT CAN BE USED RAW IN SALADS. I FIND THAT GARLIC BRINGS OUT ITS NATURAL FLAVOURS.

INGREDIENTS

Serves 2 as a main dish
  or 4 as a side dish

Preparation time: 15 minutes

Cooking time: 8 to 10 minutes

1 tbsp vegetable or sunflower oil

4 garlic cloves, peeled and crushed

900 g/2 lb a-choy

3 tbsp vegetable stock

2 tsp cornflour

METHOD

1 In a frying pan or wok heat the oil and fry the garlic for 1 minute or until just starting to brown.

2 Add the a-choy and stir fry for about 2 to 3 minutes or until slightly wilted. The colour should have intensified.

3 Add the stock. Mix the cornflour with 1 tablespoon of water and add to the pan to thicken.

4 Bring to the boil, remove from the heat and serve immediately.

OLD MAN LONG BEANS

I HAVE GIVEN THIS RECIPE ITS NAME BECAUSE THE LONG BEANS ARE WRINKLED LIKE THE SKIN OF AN OLD MAN. IT IS A QUICK AND EASY 'DRY COOK' VERSION OF LONG BEANS THAT I AM CERTAIN YOU WILL LOVE.

INGREDIENTS

Serves 4

Preparation time: 15 minutes

Cooking time: 10 minutes

1½ tbsp vegetable or sunflower oil

450 g/1 lb long beans, cut into
   5 cm/2 in lengths

3 cloves garlic, peeled and chopped

1 tbsp root ginger, peeled and chopped

1 tsp freshly ground black pepper

2 tsp dark soy sauce

Freshly ground black pepper, to serve

METHOD

1. Heat a wok or pan on a high heat and add the oil to coat the pan.
When the pan is very hot add the long beans.

2. Stir fry until wrinkled and lightly browned, for about 4 to 5 minutes.

3. Add the garlic, root ginger, pepper, and stir fry for another 1 or 2 minutes,
or until the garlic is brown.

4. Add the soy sauce and toss quickly for about 30 seconds, then serve immediately,
sprinkled with ground black pepper.

CHINESE LEAVES WITH MUSHROOMS

MY MOTHER HAD A HOST OF WAYS TO USE CHINESE LEAVES, ALL OF THEM DELICIOUS. HERE IS ONE OF THOSE RECIPES - SIMPLE YET DIVINE WHETHER YOU USE SHIITAKE MUSHROOMS OR A COMBINATION OF OYSTER, ENOKI, AND STRAW MUSHROOMS.

INGREDIENTS

Serves 4

Preparation time: 25 minutes

Cooking time: 15 minutes

6 dried or fresh shiitake mushrooms

2 tbsp vegetable or sunflower oil

2.5 cm/1 in piece root ginger, peeled and sliced

1 tsp soy sauce

125 ml/4 fl oz vegetable stock

1 tbsp oyster sauce

2 tsp cornflour

300 g/10 oz Chinese leaves, julienned

1 tbsp toasted sesame seeds, to garnish

METHOD

1. If using dried mushrooms, rinse them with water and leave to soak in enough boiling water to cover for about 20 minutes. Drain and dry with kitchen paper, cut into halves and remove the woody stems. Keep the soaking liquid. If using fresh mushrooms, rinse them in water, drain and dry with kitchen paper and cut into halves and remove the woody stems.

2. Heat one tablespoon of the oil in a pan and cook the root ginger for about 1 to 2 minutes or until it has browned.

3. Add the mushrooms and sauté for 2 to 3 minutes. Add the soy sauce, the reserved soaking liquid (or the stock), and the oyster sauce and bring to the boil. Stir in the cornflour mixed with one tablespoon of water to thicken, then set aside.

4. Heat another tablespoon of oil in a pan and stir fry the Chinese leaves for 2 to 3 minutes. Cover and cook for 2 minutes more, then remove the cover and continue to simmer for a further 2 minutes or until tender.

5. Arrange the leaves on a plate and pour the mushrooms and sauce over them. Sprinkle with toasted sesame seeds to serve.

HOT AND SOUR MUSTARD GREENS

MY MOTHER FIRST MADE THIS DISH WHEN WE WERE YOUNG
CHILDREN AND TO THIS DAY, MY BROTHER AND I REMAIN FANS OF
ITS SPICY AND SOUR FLAVOURS. HERE IS A VERSION OF MY
MOTHER'S ORIGINAL RECIPE: I HOPE YOU ENJOY IT AS MUCH AS
WE DID. ADJUST THE AMOUNT OF CHILLIES TO SUIT YOUR PALATE.

INGREDIENTS

Serves 4

Preparation time: 10 minutes

Cooking time: 40 to 45 minutes

Salt and freshly ground black pepper

1 kg/2 lb **swatow or bamboo mustard
greens, cut into bite-sized pieces**

2 tbsp vegetable or sunflower oil

1 clove garlic, peeled and chopped

**2 red bird's eye chillies,
or 1 tsp chili flakes**

**225 ml/8 fl oz Chinese vinegar or cider
vinegar**

METHOD

1   Blanch the mustard greens by covering them in slightly salted boiling water for one
minute. Remove and then plunge them into icy cold water to retain their colour and
texture. Set aside.

2   In a large pan, heat the oil, add the garlic and chillies and sauté for 3 minutes
over a medium heat.

3   Add the greens and turn the heat to high. Stir fry until the greens wilt,
adding a tablespoon of water if they dry out.

4   Reduce the heat and simmer for 30 minutes.

5   Add the vinegar, salt and pepper. Turn off the heat and let the dish stand
for 10 minutes before serving.

ROOT VEGETABLES AU GRATIN

THIS DISH TAKES ITS INFLUENCE FROM EUROPEAN STYLES OF COOKING, BUT MAKES A DELICIOUS CHANGE FROM TRADITIONAL ROOT VEGETABLE DISHES WITH THE ADDITION OF ASIAN GREENS.

INGREDIENTS

Serves 4

Preparation time: 25 minutes

Cooking time: 1 hour 30 minutes

225 g/8 oz kohlrabi, chopped

450 g/1 lb daikon, chopped

350 g/12 oz carrots, chopped

225 g/8 oz new potatoes, chopped

150g/5 oz grated cheese

3 tbsp plain flour

Salt and pepper to taste

225 ml/8 fl oz single cream

225 ml/8 fl oz milk

METHOD

1   Preheat the oven to 180°C/350°F/Gas mark 4.

2   In a large pan of salted water, bring the kohlrabi to a boil for about 3 to 4 minutes. Remove with a slotted spoon and set aside.

3   In the same pan, boil the daikon for 3 to 4 minutes. Remove with a slotted spoon and set aside.

4   Follow the same procedure for the carrots and potatoes, boiling them for 3 to 4 minutes.

5   Pat all the vegetables dry with kitchen paper and mix them together in a bowl with three-quarters of the cheese, flour, salt and pepper.

6   Spray a shallow ovenproof dish with cooking spray. Arrange the vegetables in the dish and pour the cream and milk evenly over them. Sprinkle the remaining cheese on top.

7   Bake in the oven, covered, for 30 minutes then bake, uncovered, for another 30 minutes or until the sauce is bubbling and the cheese is golden brown.

BURDOCK IN SWEET SAUCE

THIS IS ANOTHER TRADITIONAL JAPANESE RECIPE I HAVE ADOPTED FROM MY AUNT. I HAVE SPICED IT UP A LITTLE BY ADDING ROOT GINGER AND CARROTS FOR FLAVOUR AND COLOUR. I'M SURE MY AUNT WOULDN'T MIND!

INGREDIENTS

Serves 4 as a side dish

Preparation time: 20 minutes

Cooking time: 12 to 15 minutes

2 stalks burdock (celeriac can be used as an alternative), julienned

2 tsp fresh root ginger, peeled and julienned

1 small carrot, peeled and julienned

225 ml/8 fl oz dashi or stock

5 tbsp soy sauce

4 tsp mirin

2 tbsp sake

2 tbsp toasted poppy seeds, to serve

METHOD

1. In a pan, combine the burdock, root ginger, carrot and stock.
   Bring to the boil and then lower the heat to simmer for about 5 minutes.

2. Add the soy sauce, mirin and sake, simmer for another 5 to 6 minutes or until the liquid has been absorbed.

3. Remove from the heat, sprinkle with poppy seeds and serve.

SIMMERED SQUASH

SQUASH IS FILLING AND FLAVOURSOME AND IS EXCELLENT EATEN WARM OR COLD, SERVED ALONGSIDE MEAT OR ON ITS OWN. CHILDREN LOVE ITS SLIGHTLY SWEET TASTE AND I FIND ITS MELT-IN-THE-MOUTH TEXTURE SIMPLY IRRESISTIBLE.

INGREDIENTS

Serves 4

Preparation time: 5 minutes

Cooking time: 30 minutes

225 g/8 oz kabocha squash, peeled and cut into bite-sized pieces

400 ml/14 fl oz dashi or stock

2 tbsp sugar

2 tbsp mirin

1 tsp salt

1 tbsp soy sauce

Chopped parsley and freshly ground black pepper, to garnish

METHOD

1   Combine the squash, dashi, sugar, mirin and salt, cover and cook over a medium heat until tender, about 20 to 30 minutes.

2   Add the soy sauce and cook uncovered over a low heat until the liquid has almost all been absorbed. Take care when handling the squash as it will fall apart easily.

3   Remove from the heat, sprinkle with parsley and black pepper and serve.

CHOY SUM AND TOFU (BEAN CURD)
TOSSED WITH CHILLI AND SESAME SEEDS

ALTHOUGH I AM NOT A VEGETARIAN. I DO ENJOY MEATLESS DISHES. THIS IS ONE OF MY FAVOURITES. ESPECIALLY WHEN SERVED WITH STEAMING HOT RICE. IT MAKES FOR AN EXTREMELY SATISFYING LUNCH ON ITS OWN OR SERVED AS AN ACCOMPANIMENT. ADJUST THE CHILLIES TO SUIT YOUR TASTE.

INGREDIENTS

Serves 4

Preparation time: 20 minutes

Cooking time: 8 minutes

2 tbsp oyster sauce

2 tsp soy sauce

2 tbsp vegetable or sunflower oil

2 cloves garlic, peeled and crusheded

2 tsp root ginger, peeled and chopped

**2 small red chillies,
  seeded and sliced finely**

1 small red pepper, julienned

**1 bunch choy sum,
  cut into 5 cm/2 in lengths**

8 long beans, cut into 5 cm/2 in lengths

**175 g/6 oz fried tofu (bean curd),
  halved diagonally**

1 tsp sesame seeds, to serve

METHOD

1 Combine the oyster sauce and soy sauce with 1 tablespoon of water and set aside.

2 Heat the oil in a wok or frying pan, add the garlic, root ginger and chillies and fry for 1 to 2 minutes.

3 Add the red pepper, choy sum and beans. Stir fry until the choy sum has slightly wilted and the beans and pepper are slightly soft, about 2 minutes.

4 Add the tofu (bean curd) and oyster sauce mixture, toss for 3 to 4 minutes.

5 Remove from the heat, sprinkle with sesame seeds and serve.

SPICED DRUMSTICK LEAVES

IN THE PHILIPPINES. DRUMSTICK LEAVES ARE ADDED TO SOUPS AT THE VERY LAST MINUTE TO PROVIDE THE MEAL WITH A QUOTA OF GREENS. THE LEAVES COOK VERY QUICKLY AND TAKE ON A UNIQUE SLIPPERY TEXTURE. HERE. I HAVE ADDED AN INDIAN TOUCH BY USING TURMERIC AND CUMIN.

INGREDIENTS

Serves 4

Preparation time: 10 minutes

Cooking time: 15 minutes

1 tsp vegetable or sunflower oil

1 medium onion, diced

1 tsp turmeric

1 tsp ground cumin

1 tsp salt

Juice of 1 lime

4 tbsp dessicated coconut (optional)

175g/6 oz drumstick leaves

METHOD

1 Heat the oil in a pan and fry the diced onion for 1 minute.

2 Add the turmeric, cumin and salt, and stir for about 30 seconds to 1 minute or until fragrant.

3 Stir in the lime juice, flaked coconut if using, add 3 tablespoons of water and cook, covered, for 10 minutes.

4 Add the drumstick leaves and cook, uncovered, for about 5 minutes or until the liquid has evaporated. Serve immediately.

FLASH FRIED PEA SPROUTS

NORMALLY, THIS RECIPE WILL FEED FOUR HUNGRY PEOPLE. HOWEVER, WHEN MY BROTHER AND I ARE AT THE SAME TABLE, IT WILL ONLY FEED THE TWO OF US, WE SIMPLY LOVE OUR GREENS!

INGREDIENTS

Serves 4
Preparation time: 5 minutes
Cooking time: 5 to 6 minutes

1 tbsp vegetable
  or sunflower oil

450 g/1 lb small pea sprouts,
  rinsed and drained well

⅕ tsp Chinese
  five-spice powder

1 tbsp light soy sauce

2 spring onions, sliced finely

METHOD

1   Heat the oil, add the pea sprouts and stir fry for 2 minutes making sure they don't burn.

2   Stir in the five-spice powder, soy sauce, and spring onions. Stir fry for 2 to 3 minutes and serve immediately.

LETTUCE STEM IN SESAME OIL

LETTUCE STEM IS A COMMON STAPLE FOR NORTHERN CHINESE PEOPLE AND WHEN I FIRST TASTED IT IN HONG KONG AS A TEENAGER, I BECAME AN AVID FAN.

INGREDIENTS

Serves 4 as a side dish
Preparation time: 20 minutes
Cooking time: 5 minutes

6 stalks lettuce stem,
  cut into chunks

2 tbsp sesame oil

1 tbsp light soy sauce

METHOD

1   Parboil the lettuce stem in a pan of boiling water for 2 minutes. Remove and plunge into icy cold water. Set aside.

2   When the lettuce stem has cooled, toss with the sesame oil until well coated. Add the soy sauce and toss again. Refrigerate for at least 2 hours and serve chilled.

SESAME EGGPLANT

A JAPANESE FRIEND OF MINE MAKES THIS VERSATILE DISH AS AN APPETIZER TO BE EATEN AT ROOM TEMPERATURE. I PREFER TO SERVE IT HOT AND AS A SIDE DISH TO MAIN COURSES. EITHER WAY IT IS DELICIOUS.

INGREDIENTS

*Serves 4 as an appetizer,
  2 as a main dish*

Preparation time: 5 minutes

Cooking time: 10 to 15 minutes

2 eggplants, roughly 300 g/10 oz each

Vegetable or sunflower oil for frying

225 ml/8 fl oz vegetable stock

1½ tbsp sugar

1 tbsp soy sauce

1½ tsp cornflour

3 tbsp sesame seeds, to garnish

METHOD

1   Peel the eggplants and cut each of them into six pieces lengthwise. Soak in water for about 15 minutes, drain, and place on kitchen paper to absorb the remaining water.

2   Heat the oil to 150-200°C/350-400°F and fry the eggplant on both sides until golden brown. Transfer to kitchen paper to drain off any excess oil.

3   Place the eggplant and stock in a pan, bring to the boil, then reduce the heat to a simmer and add the sugar. Simmer for about 1 to 2 minutes.

4   Mix the soy sauce with the cornflour and add to the pan, stirring continuously until the sauce thickens.

5   Sprinkle with sesame seeds and serve.

3 | MEAT AND POULTRY

VEGETABLE AND CHICKEN HOT POT

THIS IS AN INTIMATE ONE-POT MEAL FOR TWO ON DAYS YOU DON'T REALLY FEEL LIKE COOKING OR EATING OUT. IF PREFERRED YOU CAN EXCHANGE SLICED BEEF FOR CHICKEN OR USE BOTH FOR A HEARTIER MEAL.

INGREDIENTS

Serves 2

Preparation time: 30 minutes

Cooking time: 15 minute

450 ml/16 fl oz dashi or vegetable stock

120 ml/4 fl oz soy sauce

120 ml/4 fl oz mirin

1 leek, white part only,
 cut into 2.5 cm/1 in lengths

1 medium piece jicama, diced

6 fresh shiitake mushrooms,
 stems discarded

1 choy sum floret or baby bok choy,
 split lengthways

225 g/8 oz chicken breast, boneless,
 skinless, cubed

175 g/6 oz firm tofu (bean curd), cubed

1 large carrot, peeled and diced

120 g/4 oz spinach, stems removed

1 lemon, sliced into wedges, to serve

METHOD

1 Combine the dashi or stock with 225 ml/8 fl oz water, the soy sauce, and the mirin in a pan and bring to the boil, then reduce the heat to a simmer.

2 Meanwhile arrange all the remaining ingredients, except the spinach and lemon, in a separate deep pan. Turn the heat on low and pour the simmering mixture from the other pan slowly into the deep pan. Simmer, uncovered, for about 5 minutes or until the vegetables are tender.

3 Add the spinach by pushing it into the outer edges of the pan and cook for 2 minutes.

4 Remove from the heat and squeeze lemon juice into the soup just before serving. Serve piping hot.

CHICKEN DUMPLINGS WITH CHIVES

DUMPLINGS HAVE ALWAYS BEEN A FAMILY AFFAIR AT MY HOUSE.
MY BROTHER AND I WOULD SIT DOWN AND MAKE THE LITTLE
DUMPLINGS AND HAVE MOTHER COOK THEM AS WE MADE THEM.
OF COURSE, EATING THEM WAS THE BEST PART! HERE I HAVE USED
CHICKEN INSTEAD OF PORK FOR A LEANER ALTERNATIVE.

INGREDIENTS

Serves 4

Preparation time: 20 minutes

Cooking time: 20 minutes

110 g/4 oz ground chicken

2 tbsp light soy sauce

2 tbsp ginger juice (see page 35)

$\frac{1}{4}$ tsp white pepper

$\frac{1}{2}$ tsp Shaoxing wine or dry sherry

$1\frac{1}{2}$ tbsp cornflour

60 g/2 oz chives, chopped
  into $\frac{1}{2}$ inch lengths

$1\frac{1}{2}$ tbsp sesame oil

24 dumpling wrappers

Vegetable oil, for deep frying

Chilli sauce, to serve

METHOD

1 In a bowl combine the chicken, soy sauce, ginger juice, white pepper, and wine,
   mixing together well.

2 Add the cornflour and mix well, then set aside for at least an hour in the refrigerator.

3 In another bowl, mix the chopped chives and sesame oil, then set aside.

4 Just before starting to wrap the dumplings, mix together the chicken mixture
   and the chive mixture until thoroughly combined.

5 Place about one teaspoon of the filling onto a dumpling wrapper, brush the edges with a
   little water and pinch them closed. Repeat until the filling is used up.

6 Heat a wok or frying pan and add oil to a depth of about 10 cm/4 in. Heat the oil to
   190° C/375°F. Deep fry the dumplings, a few at a time, and turning them as they fry, for 3 to 4
   minutes or until golden and crisp. Drain on kitchen paper. Chicken dumplings can also be
   boiled for 5 to 6 minutes or steamed for 15 minutes.

7 Serve the dumplings with chili sauce.

STUFFED FUZZY MELON

THIS DISH IS TRADITIONALLY MADE WITH CONPOY (DRIED SCALLOPS) BUT I HAVE SUBSTITUTED SHIITAKE MUSHROOMS FOR A RICHER FLAVOUR. I SOMETIMES USE GROUND TURKEY INSTEAD OF THE PORK IN THIS RECIPE.

INGREDIENTS

Serves 4

Preparation time: 25 minutes

Cooking time: 10 to 15 minutes

225 g/8 oz ground pork

5 tbsp light soy sauce

4 tbsp ginger juice (see page 35)

2 tsp Shaoxing wine or dry sherry

$\frac{1}{2}$ tsp white pepper

3 tbsp cornflour

6 large fresh or dried shiitake mushrooms, soaked (if using dried) and diced

4 water chestnuts, peeled and diced

2 large fuzzy melons

METHOD

1 In a bowl, combine the pork, soy, ginger juice, wine and white pepper. Mix well.

2 Add in the cornflour and mix well until blended, then add the mushrooms and water chestnuts, and mix until well combined.

3 Cut the fuzzy melons lengthways, scoop out the seeds and spongy middle section to create a valley. Stuff the pork mixture into the valley. Alternatively, cut the fuzzy melons into five sections widthways so they look like little cylinders. Scoop out the spongy part and stuff with the pork mixture.

4 Place into a steamer with boiling water and steam for 8 to 10 minutes or until the melon has softened. Serve immediately.

SPICY BEEF WITH CHINESE CELERY

I LOVE COOKING WITH AROMATIC CHINESE CELERY BECAUSE IT COMPLEMENTS EVERYTHING IT IS COOKED WITH. I HAVE ADDED CHILLIES TO THIS RECIPE BUT IF YOU PREFER NOT TO, IT WILL NOT IMPAIR THE DELIGHTFUL FLAVOURS OF THIS DISH.

INGREDIENTS

Serves 4

Preparation time 20 minutes

Cooking time 6 to 8 minutes

450 g/1 lb flank steak, cut into fine strips

2 tbsp dark soy sauce

1 tsp Shaoxing wine or dry sherry

2 tsp root ginger, peeled and chopped

4 tbsp vegetable or sunflower oil

3 medium carrots, julienned

12 stalks Chinese celery, julienned, leaves included

1-3 tsp red chillies, or chilli flakes

$\frac{1}{4}$ tsp salt

1 tsp cornflour

1 tsp chilli flakes, to garnish

METHOD

1   Marinate the steak with the soy sauce, wine and root ginger. Set aside in the refrigerator for at least 30 minutes.

2   Heat the oil over a high heat and cook the beef, stirring for about 2 to 3 minutes, until browned. Remove with a slotted spoon and set aside.

3   In the same pan, cook the carrots for 1 minute, add the celery, chillies and salt and stir for 1 minute.

4   Return the beef to the pan and stir fry for about 1 minute.

5   Mix the cornflour with one tablespoon of water and add to the pan to thicken. Bring to the boil, toss and serve, sprinkled with chilli flakes.

BEEF BRISKET STEW WITH DAIKON

IN NORTHERN CHINA, THIS DISH IS TRADITIONALLY EATEN DURING
WINTER AND CUSTOMARILY PREPARED IN A CLAYPOT SO IT WILL
RETAIN ITS HEAT. CARROTS AND OTHER ROOT VEGETABLES SUCH
AS KOHLRABI, TURNIPS AND PARSNIPS CAN ALSO BE ADDED.

INGREDIENTS

Serves 4

Preparation time: 30 minutes

Cooking time: 1 hour 15 minutes

5 pieces root ginger, (2.5 cm/1 in thick),
  peeled

6 spring onions, chopped

2 tbsp vegetable or sunflower oil

3 cloves garlic, peeled and crushed

3 star anise

1 cinnamon stick

1 tbsp Shaoxing wine or dry sherry

1.8 l/3¼ pts chicken stock

5 tbsp dark soy sauce

5 tbsp light brown sugar

225 g/8 oz beef brisket

450 g/1 lb daikon, peeled,
  cut into similar size chunks

1 tbsp cornflour

Chilli oil, to taste

Salt, to taste

1 spring onion, chopped finely

METHOD

1   Heat a pan of water large enough to fit the entire brisket. When the water is boiling, put
    in one piece of root ginger and two spring onions and cook with the brisket for
    20 minutes in the water. Drain the meat and cut into 2.5 cm/1 in cubes and set aside.

2   Heat the oil in a large pan and fry the remaining root ginger and spring onions for about
    2 minutes. Add the garlic and cook for about 30 seconds.

3   Add the star anise, cinnamon, wine, stock, soy sauce, brown sugar, beef and daikon,
    bring to the boil, reduce the heat and simmer for about 30 to 40 minutes, or until
    the beef and daikon are tender. Remove the spices from the pan.

4   If desired, add salt to taste. Thicken the sauce with the cornflour, mixed with
    two teaspoons of water and a dash of chilli oil. Serve hot, sprinkled with chopped
    spring onions.

CHICKEN WITH THAI BASIL

AFTER FALLING IN LOVE WITH THIS RECIPE MANY YEARS AGO. IT HAS BECOME ONE OF MY FAVOURITE THAI DISHES. THIS IS MY OWN VERSION. AFTER NUMEROUS SAMPLINGS IN RESTAURANTS IN HONG KONG AND THAILAND. I SUGGEST SERVING IT WITH STEAMING HOT JASMINE RICE.

INGREDIENTS

Serves 4

Preparation time: 15 minutes

Cooking time: 10 minutes

450 g/1 lb chicken breasts, boneless, skinless, cubed

4 tbsp fish sauce

3 tbsp vegetable or sunflower oil

4 garlic cloves, peeled and sliced

2-4 red chillies, seeded and chopped

2 tsp dark soy sauce

½ tsp sugar

15 Thai basil leaves

METHOD

1 Marinate the chicken in three tablespoons of the fish sauce, and set aside for at least 30 minutes.

2 Heat the oil in a frying pa and fry the garlic and chillies until golden, about 2 to 3 minutes.

3 Add the chicken and fry until slightly browned, about 2 to 3 minutes.

4 Add the remaining fish sauce, soy sauce, and sugar. Stir for about 3 to 4 minutes or until well cooked.

5 Stir in the basil leaves, cook for a further 1 minute and serve immediately.

HAM WITH SHALLOTS
AND BALSAMIC VINEGAR

THIS RECIPE SHOULD BE SERVED WITH SCRAMBLED EGGS OR ANOTHER BREAKFAST ITEM, OR YOU CAN SERVE IT WITH FRITTATA AND MUFFINS FOR A FILLING SUNDAY BRUNCH. WHETHER IT IS EATEN WARM OR AT ROOM TEMPERATURE, IT WILL STILL TASTE DIVINE.

INGREDIENTS

Serves 4

Preparation time: 5 minutes

Cooking time: 6 to 8 minutes

1 tbsp olive oil

3 shallots, peeled and chopped

120 g/4 oz smoked ham, cut into strips

3 tbsp balsamic vinegar

2 tbsp Chinese celery, chopped

METHOD

1 Heat the oil in a heavy frying pan, add the shallots and cook for 2 minutes over a medium heat. Add the balsamic vinegar and two tablespoons of water, and cook until reduced by half, about 1 to 2 minutes.

2 Add the ham and cook for 3 to 4 minutes or until well mixed, making sure the caramelized vinegar does not burn.

3 Add the celery and stir for about 2 minutes or until wilted. Serve immediately.

BRAISED PORK WITH CHAYOTE

THIS VEGETABLE IS IDEAL WHEN USED FOR BRAISING OR STEWS BECAUSE IT COOKS WELL. I ADD OTHER ROOT VEGETABLES FOR MORE FLAVOUR AND RICHER COLOUR, ESPECIALLY WHEN I AM ENTERTAINING FRIENDS.

INGREDIENTS

Serves 4

Preparation time: 20 minutes

Cooking time: 35 to 40 minutes

450 g/1 lb pork tenderloin,
　cut into 2.5 cm/$\frac{1}{2}$ inch pieces

2 cloves garlic, peeled and crushed

2.5 cm/1 in piece root ginger,
　peeled and minced

$\frac{1}{2}$ tsp salt

2 tbsp Shaoxing wine or dry sherry

1 tbsp cornflour

$\frac{1}{2}$ tsp vegetable or sunflower oil

3 medium chayotes, peeled
　and cut into 1 cm/$\frac{1}{2}$ in cubes

225 ml/8 fl oz stock

$\frac{1}{2}$ tsp fish sauce

$\frac{1}{2}$ tsp sugar

$\frac{1}{4}$ tsp white pepper

METHOD

1　Marinate the pork with the garlic, root ginger, salt, wine and cornflour
　for at least 30 minutes.

2　Heat the oil in a pan and fry the pork until golden brown. Remove and keep warm
　in a low oven.

3　Add the chayote to the pan and fry for 1 minute, then add the stock
　and bring to the boil.

4　Add the fish sauce, sugar and pepper and braise for 20 minutes over a low heat
　or until the chayote is tender.

5　Turn the heat to high, return the pork to the pan and stir until the sauce has slightly
　thickened. Serve immediately.

SPICED TOFU AND LONG BEANS
WITH TURKEY

DELICIOUS AND FILLING. THIS ALONE IS ENOUGH TO SATISFY ME
WHEN SERVED WITH SOME STEAMING WHITE RICE. FOR AN EXTRA
KICK, ADD A TEASPOON OF CHILLI OIL BEFORE SERVING..

INGREDIENTS

Serves 4

Preparation time: 15 minutes

Cooking time: 10 minutes

150 g/5 oz long beans, cut into
  2.5 cm/1 in lengths

120 g/4 oz ground turkey

¼ tsp cornflour

50 g/2 oz bean sprouts

2 tbsp vegetable or sunflower oil

1 tbsp Shaoxing wine or dry sherry

120 g/4 oz spiced tofu (bean curd), diced

1 clove garlic, peeled and crushed

For the sauce

1 tsp oyster sauce

1 tsp light soy sauce

¼ tsp sugar

½ tsp cornflour

METHOD

1 Blanch the long beans by covering them in boiling water for 30 seconds,
then plunging them into icy water. Drain and set aside.

2 Mix the turkey with the cornflour and one teaspoon of water, and set it aside.

3 Fry the bean sprouts in a pan in one tablespoon of oil and the wine. Remove them with
a slotted spoon and set aside.

4 Heat another tablespoon of oil in a wok and fry the crushed garlic. Add the turkey and
stir fry until lightly browned, about 3 minutes. Add the long beans and cook for another 2
to 3 minutes or until beans are cooked through.

5 Meanwhile combine all the ingredients for the sauce in a bowl. Add the bean sprouts and
spiced tofu (bean curd) to the pan and stir for about 30 seconds. Add the sauce and
bring to the boil, cooking until the sauce has thickened. Serve immediately with a bowl
of hot rice.

ASIAN-STYLE BOLOGNAISE

MY MOTHER SERVES THIS OVER PLAIN NOODLE SOUP OR JUST
NOODLES AS ONE WOULD SERVE PASTA IN ITALIAN CUISINE.
I PREFER THIN SOBA NOODLES BUT YOU COULD USE THICKER
UDON NOODLES. YOU CAN ALSO SUBSTITUTE GROUND BEEF FOR
TURKEY IF YOU PREFER A LEANER MEAT.

INGREDIENTS

Serves 4

Preparation time: 20 minutes

Cooking time: 10 minutes

450 g/1 lb ground turkey

3 tbsp light soy sauce

1 tbsp ginger juice (see page 35)

1 tbsp vegetable or sunflower oil

120 g/4 oz celery leaf, chopped

1 tbsp oyster sauce

1 tsp cornflour

Noodles (udon, soba), to serve

METHOD

1   Combine the turkey, soy sauce and ginger juice. Mix well and allow to marinate
for at least 30 minutes.

2   Heat the oil over a high heat in a pan. Add the turkey mixture and stir for about
2 to 3 minutes, or until browned. Remove the turkey mixture with a slotted spoon and set
it aside.

3   Add the celery and stir for about 1 to 2 minutes or until the celery has
softened slightly.

4   Return the turkey to the pan, add the oyster sauce and stir quickly until combined
thoroughly.

5   Mix the cornflour with one tablespoon of water and add it to the pan, then bring
to the boil to thicken the sauce. Serve immediately with your choice of noodles.

NEW AGE LION'S HEAD WITH BOK CHOY

TRADITIONALLY MADE WITH A MIX OF FAT AND PORK, THIS NORTHERN CHINESE DISH GAVE ITS PEOPLE ADDED CALORIES TO HELP THEM ENDURE THE HARSH WINTERS. MY MOTHER MADE IT WITH GROUND LEAN PORK, BUT I PREFER TURKEY, OR A COMBINATION OF THE TWO.

INGREDIENTS

Serves 4

Preparation time: 30 minutes

Cooking time: 1 hour 15 minutes

450 g/ 1 lb ground turkey

2 tbsp dark soy sauce

1 tbsp light soy sauce

1 tbsp ginger juice (see page 35)

1 cm/½ in piece root ginger, peeled and chopped

2 tbsp breadcrumbs, plain

2 tsp cornflour

Vegetable or sunflower oil for frying

3 tbsp dark soy sauce

450 ml/16 fl oz chicken stock

3 tbsp light brown sugar

Extra 1 tbsp cornflour

6 stalks Shanghai bok choy, ends cut to separate leaves

METHOD

1   Mix together the first seven ingredients until thoroughly blended. Marinate for at least 3 hours (but preferably overnight) in the refrigerator.

2   Separate the mixture into four and roll it between your palms to form rounds the size of tennis balls.

3   Heat enough oil in a frying pan to cover about a third of the base of the pan. Brown the outside of the meatballs and set them aside.

4   In a heavy-bottomed pan, place the meatballs, dark soy, chicken stock and brown sugar, and bring to the boil. Turn the heat down to medium-high and leave for 45 minutes or until the liquid has reduced by half, occasionally turning the meatballs over.

5   Combine one tablespoon of cornflour mixed with one tablespoon of water, add to the sauce and stir until it thickens. Tuck the bok choy leaves around the meatballs and simmer for 4 to 5 minutes or until the bok choy is tender. Serve piping hot.

ASIAN BREAKFAST FRITTATA

THIS IS A SIMPLE DISH THAT IS GOOD AT ANY TIME OF THE DAY, BUT ESPECIALLY FOR BREAKFAST, AS MITSUBA IS GREAT WITH EGGS. DO NOT USE HERBS IN THIS RECIPE AS THEY WILL NOT COMPLEMENT THE EGGS. HERE, LESS IS MORE!

INGREDIENTS

Serves 4

Preparation time: 7 minutes

Cooking time: 25 to 30 minutes

2 medium potatoes, chopped finely

5 tbsp milk

2 tbsp Parmesan cheese, grated

5 extra large eggs

3 extra large egg whites

120 g/4 oz cooked ham or turkey, chopped

120 g/4 oz mitsuba, ends trimmed

Salt and freshly ground black pepper, to taste

2 tsp butter

5 tbsp grated mozzarella cheese

METHOD

1 Preheat the grill and set at a medium heat.

2 In a pan of salted water, boil the potatoes for 8 to 10 minutes or until soft.
   Drain and set them aside.

3 Combine the milk, Parmesan cheese, eggs and egg whites and mix with a whisk.
   Add the potatoes, the ham or turkey and the mitsuba and combine well.
   Add salt and pepper to taste.

4 In a non-stick frying pan, melt the butter over a medium heat and add the egg mixture.

5 Cook slowly being careful not to burn the bottom of the frittata. Turn the heat down a notch if necessary. Cook for 10 to 15 minutes or until the top has started to set.

6 Sprinkle the top with mozzarella and place under the grill for 3 to 5 minutes, or until golden brown. Serve.

GRILLED BEEF
ON CHRYSANTHEMUM LEAVES

IN THAILAND. THIS DISH IS SERVED WITH WESTERN SALAD ITEMS. I USE WHATEVER VEGETABLE I HAVE AND FOUND THAT THE FRAGRANT AROMA OF CHRYSANTHEMUM LEAVES MAKES A DELIGHTFUL ACCOMPANIMENT TO GRILLED BEEF.

INGREDIENTS

Serves 2

Preparation time: 15 minutes
  (plus 2 hours marinating time)

Cooking time: 15 minutes

5 cloves garlic, peeled and chopped

4 shallots, peeled and chopped

1 stalk lemongrass, heart only

1 tbsp Chinese cooking wine
  or dry sherry

1 tbsp soy sauce

2 tbsp fish sauce

2 tsp sugar

450 g/1 lb beef, any tender cut

120 g/4 oz chrysanthemum leaves

For the dressing

Juice of 1 lime

Juice of 1 lemon

1 fresh chilli, sliced or chilli
  flakes, to garnish (optional)

1 tbsp fish sauce

3 tsp sugar

METHOD

1   In a blender or food processor, puree the garlic, shallots, lemongrass, wine, soy sauce, fish sauce and sugar until well blended. Marinate the beef in the blended mixture in a zip-lock plastic bag for at least two hours, but preferably overnight in the refrigerator.

2   Blanch the chrysanthemum leaves by covering them in four cups of salted, boiling water, then plunge them into icy water to retain their colour and texture. Drain and squeeze the excess water from the leaves and set aside.

3   Grill the beef for 5 to 7 minutes per side to serve rare. With a sharp knife, cut the meat into fine strips against the grain, and set aside.

4   In a small bowl or jar, mix the dressing ingredients together and toss with the leaves. Arrange the leaves on a plate, lay the sliced beef on top and serve garnished with sliced chillies or chilli flakes. Can be served warm or at room temperature.

4 FISH

SPICY PRAWNS WITH LONG BEANS

A FILIPINO FRIEND MADE A VERSION OF THIS DISH TO WHICH I HAVE ADAPTED CERTAIN INGREDIENTS. I FIND THAT COCONUT MILK GIVES THIS DISH A SLIGHTLY RICHER FLAVOUR. BUT AS IT'S HIGH ON FAT. YOU MIGHT CHOOSE TO LEAVE IT OUT

INGREDIENTS

Serves 4

Preparation time: 15 minutes

Cooking time: 5 minutes

2 large dried red chillies, chopped finely or 2 tsp chilli flakes

4 large shallots, peeled and chopped

½ tsp shrimp paste or anchovy paste

2 tbsp vegetable or sunflower oil

2 tbsp peanuts, crushed

225 g/8 oz prawns, raw, peeled

225 g/8 oz long beans, cut into 2.5 cm/1 in lengths

120 ml/4 fl oz coconut milk

¼ tsp salt

1 tsp sugar

METHOD

1 With a mortar and pestle or food processor, mix the chillies, shallots and shrimp or anchovy paste together.

2 Heat the oil in a frying pan and fry the mixture until fragrant, about 1 minute.

3 Add the peanuts and prawns. Stir well.

4 Add the long beans, coconut milk, salt and sugar. Stir well for about 1 minute.

5 When everything is well coated, serve with steaming rice.

SPICY SCALLOP LETTUCE WRAPS

I HAVE ADAPTED THIS DISH USING SCALLOPS AND GROUND TURKEY IN PLACE OF THE PIGEON WHICH IS USED IN ASIA. INSTEAD OF BUTTERHEAD LETTUCE. YOU COULD TRY USING ROMAINE OR RED-LEAF LETTUCE. OR A COMBINATION.

INGREDIENTS

Serves 4

Preparation time: 15 minutes

Cooking time: 10 minutes

225 g/8 oz small scallops

2 ½ tsp cornflour

1 egg white

Salt and freshly ground black pepper

90 g/3 oz ground turkey

1 tsp light soy sauce

5 tsp vegetable or sunflower oil

120 g/4 oz celery leaf, chopped

8 water chestnuts, chopped

120 g/4 oz bamboo shoots, chopped

1 clove garlic, peeled and crushed

1 tsp root ginger, peeled and chopped

2 spring onions, sliced finely

16 butterhead lettuce leaves,
    washed and dried on kitchen paper

½ tbsp chilli bean sauce, to serve

METHOD

1   Blanch the scallops by covering them with boiling water for 10 seconds. Remove and plunge them into icy water and drain. Marinate the scallops in two teaspoons cornflour, the egg white, and salt and pepper and set aside for at least 30 minutes.

2   Marinate the ground turkey in the remaining cornflour, light soy sauce, one teaspoon of water and one teaspoon of oil and set aside for at least 30 minutes.

3   Drain the turkey, reserving the marinade. Heat the remaining oil in a frying pan and fry the turkey until almost cooked through. Add the celery, water chestnuts, bamboo shoots, garlic, root ginger and spring onions, mixing well for about 2 to 3 minutes.

4   Add the scallops and cook for 1 minute before adding the reserved marinade. Mix thoroughly, and cook until the sauce boils and thickens.

5   Place a tablespoon of the scallop mixture on each lettuce leaf and serve with chilli bean sauce on the side.

SLOW COOKED SALMON
WITH ASIAN GREENS

THIS RECIPE COMES FROM PETER FIND, CHEF AT THE RITZ-CARLTON HOTEL, MILLENIA SINGAPORE. HIS RECIPE FOR SLOW COOKED SALMON ABSOLUTELY MELTS IN THE MOUTH. I'VE MADE A FEW CHANGES TO MAKE IT EASIER FOR HOME COOKING, BUT THE FINAL CREDIT MUST GO TO PETER.

INGREDIENTS

Serves 4

Preparation time: 30 minutes

Cooking time: 1 hour

300 g/10 oz baby bok choy, whole

Four 225 g/8 oz salmon fillets, grey parts removed

3 tbsp olive oil

Salt and freshly ground black pepper

2.5 cm/1 in piece root ginger, peeled and julienned

450 ml/16 fl oz vegetable or fish broth

300 g/10 oz bamboo shoots, julienned

300 g/10 oz shiitake mushrooms, stems removed, halved or quartered

120 g/4 oz spring onions, julienned

METHOD

1 Preheat the oven to 110°C/225°F/Gas mark ¼.

2 Blanch the baby bok choy by covering it in boiling water for 30 seconds, then plunging it in icy water. Drain and cut it in half lengthwise, then set it aside.

3 On the lowest rack of the oven, place an uncovered, ovenproof pan of hot water. The evaporating water will help to keep the fish moist while cooking. Lightly brush the salmon with the oil and season with salt and pepper. Bake in an ovenproof dish for 40 to 50 minutes, depending on how well-cooked you prefer your salmon.

4 In another pan, place the root ginger and stock, bring to the boil, add the bok choy, bamboo shoots and mushrooms. Turn the heat down to a simmer and cook for 10 minutes.

5 Ladle some stock and vegetables into a bowl making sure the root ginger remains in the pan. Place a piece of salmon over the vegetables and garnish with the cooked root ginger and the spring onions.

STEAMED SALMON
WITH ROASTED ROOT VEGETABLES

EVEN PEOPLE WHO SWEAR THEY DON'T LIKE FISH SEEM TO LOVE THIS RECIPE. PERHAPS IT'S BECAUSE SALMON IS SO MILD AND SOFT-TEXTURED. YOU CAN SUBSTITUTE ANY OILY FISH FOR THE SALMON, BUT MY FAVOURITE ALTERNATIVE IS SEA BASS.

INGREDIENTS

Serves 4

Preparation time: 30 minutes

Cooking time: 35 to 40 minutes

3 kohlrabi, peeled and cubed

4 carrots, peeled and cubed

2 chayote, peeled and cubed

3 tbsp (plus 1 tsp) olive oil

1 daikon, peeled and cubed

$\frac{1}{4}$ tsp freshly ground black pepper

1 tsp salt

Four 120 g/4 oz salmon fillets

$\frac{1}{4}$ tsp salt

2 tbsp fresh dill, chopped, to serve

METHOD

1 Preheat the oven to 190°C/375°F/Gas mark 5.

2 In a bowl, combine the vegetables with one teaspoon of oil, salt and pepper.

3 Spread the vegetables out on an ovenproof sheet and bake for 20 to 30 minutes.

4 When the vegetables have been in the oven for approximately 15 minutes, place the salmon, skin side down, in the steamer, brush the fillets with oil, and sprinkle with kosher salt and black pepper. Steam the salmon for approximately 6 minutes. Remove and serve.

5 Toss the vegetables with dill before serving. Season to taste, if necessary.

FLOWERING CHIVES WITH CLAMS

THIS DISH TAKES NO TIME AT ALL TO MAKE AND IS DELICIOUS OVER STEAMED RICE. YOU CAN SUBSTITUTE CLAMS FOR MUSSELS AND, IF YOU LIKE, ADD IN A FEW OYSTERS FOR A DECADENT TOUCH!

INGREDIENTS

Serves 4

Preparation time: 5 minutes

Cooking time: 5 minutes

1 tbsp vegetable or sunflower oil

2 cloves garlic , peeled and crushed

175 g/6 oz flowering chives,
   cut into 2.5 cm/1 in lengths

225 g/8 oz whole clams, tinned,
   or freshly cooked and shelled

1 tbsp oyster sauce

$\frac{1}{4}$ tsp sugar

1 tsp cornflour

METHOD

1   Heat the oil in a frying pan and fry the garlic for 1 minute, until lightly browned.

2   Add the chives and stir fry for 1 minute.

3   Stir in the clams, oyster sauce and sugar. Mix well.

4   Combine the cornflour with two tablespoons of water and add to the pan stirring continuously until the sauce thickens, about 2 minutes. Take care not to overcook the clams or they will toughen.

5   Serve immediately, with a bowl of steamed rice.

GINGERED PRAWNS
WITH ANGLED LOOFAH

THIS DISH IS TRADITIONALLY MADE WITH DRIED SHRIMP. I HAVE USED FRESH. BUT IF YOU WANT TO USE DRIED SHRIMPS. REDUCE THE AMOUNT GIVEN BY HALF AND OMIT THE SALT AND NUTS. THIS RECIPE IS GREAT WITH UPO. CHAYOTE. OR FUZZY MELON.

INGREDIENTS

Serves 4

Preparation time: 30 minutes

Cooking time: 10 minutes

1 tbsp vegetable or sunflower oil

1 medium onion, chopped

1 cm/½ in piece root ginger, sliced in 3

350 g/12 oz medium to large prawns, raw, peeled

3 tbsp chicken stock

1 tsp cornflour

1 tbsp Shaoxing wine or dry sherry

1 large angled loofah, cut into bite-sized chunks

¼ tsp salt

25 g/1 oz cashews or walnuts, toasted and lightly crushed

¼ tsp white pepper

METHOD

1 Heat the oil in a frying pan and fry the onion and root ginger for about 30 seconds. Add the prawns and fry for about 1 minute or until they are opaque in colour. Remove the prawns with a slotted spoon and set aside.

2 Add the stock, cornflour, and wine to the pan and bring to the boil. Add the angled loofah and salt, and braise for about 2 minutes.

3 When the liquid has reduced by half, return the prawns to the pan and add the nuts. Stir fry for about 1 to 2 minutes, then add the white pepper and serve.